Implementation of Article 82 of the United Nations Convention on the Law of the Sea

ISA TECHNICAL STUDY: No.12

International Seabed Authority

Kingston, Jamaica

NATIONAL LIBRARY OF JAMAICA CATALOGUING-IN-PUBLICATION DATA

Implementation of Article 82 of the United Nations Convention on the Law of the Sea: report of the International Workshop convened by the International Seabed Authority in collaboration with the China Institute for Marine Affairs in Beijing, the People's Republic of China, 26-30 November 2012

p. ; cm. – (Technical study; no. 12)

ISBN 978-976-8241-17-7 (pbk)

1. Law of the Sea

2. Ocean bottom – Law and legislation – International cooperation

3. Maritime law – International cooperation

I. Series

341.450268 – dc 23

Copyright © International Seabed Authority 2013

International Seabed Authority
14-20 Port Royal Street
Kingston, Jamaica
Tel: (876) 922 9105, Fax: (876) 922 0195
Website: http://www.isa.org.jm

On the cover: Photo from the International Workshop on Further Consideration of the Implementation of Article 82 of the United Nations Convention on the Law of the Sea, 26-30 November 2012, Tangla Hotel, Beijing, China.

Contents

Foreword

The present Technical Study is prepared by the Secretariat of the International Seabed Authority (the Authority) to provide a summary of the International Workshop on Further Consideration of the Implementation of Article 82 of the United Nations Convention on the Law of the Sea (the Convention), which was held in Beijing, China, from 26 to 30 November 2012 (Beijing Workshop), in collaboration with the China Institute for Marine Affairs (CIMA). The Technical Study contains opening and welcoming remarks made at the opening session, and a summary report of the workshop. The reports by Working Group A on implementation guidelines and a model agreement and Working Group B on possible options for equitable distribution of payments and contributions in-kind, and a summary of conclusions and recommendations from the workshop appear as Annexes 1, 2 and 3, respectively. The following main working papers prepared for participants in the workshop are also incorporated in the Technical Study as Annexes 4, 5 and 6: *Development of Guidelines for the Implementation of Article 82* by Professor Aldo Chircop of Marine and Environmental Law Institute, Schulich School of Law, Dalhousie University, Canada; *Exploring the Outer Continental Shelf* by Robert van de Poll, International Manager, Law of the Sea, Furgo, N.V., Leidschendam, the Netherlands and Clive Schofield, Director of Research, Australian National Centre for Ocean Resources and Security, University of Wollongong, Australia; and *Possible Options on Equitable Distribution of Payments and Contributions* by Professor Frida Armas-Pfirter, Austral University School of Law, Buenos Aires, Argentina. Other papers presented at the workshop, and referred to in the workshop programme (Appendix 1), many of which were in the form of slide presentations, are archived on the website of the Authority.

Article 76 of the Convention entitles a potential extension of a State's continental shelf to 350 nautical miles, which erodes the size of the Area and hence the resources available to developing and land-locked States. Article 82 was introduced as a quid pro quo for this situation. As part of the overall legal regime for the continental shelf established under the Convention, Article 82 is a unique provision of international law and an important component of the concept of the common heritage of mankind. Whilst the intent behind Article 82 is clear, its language leaves a number of important practical issues unresolved. Much further work remains to be done if the provisions are to be applied uniformly and consistently in State practice. In order to avoid potential future disputes over the interpretation and application of Article 82, it is important that these issues are resolved as soon as possible. Clear and unambiguous guidance as to how Article 82 will be implemented in future will also help to provide greater certainty to the offshore industry and enable it to promote more activity on the outer, or extended, continental shelf.[1]

The Authority's work on resolution of the issues associated with the implementation of Article 82 commenced with a seminar in 2009 held in collaboration with the Royal Institute of International Affairs (Chatham House) in London. As proposed by the Secretary-General in his annual report to the Assembly of the Authority during its sixteenth session in 2010, this work was included in the Authority's work programme for the period 2011-2013. Accordingly, and as a follow-up to the Chatham House seminar, the Beijing Workshop aimed to draw up recommendations for Article 82 implementation guidelines and the outline of a model Article 82 agreement between the ISA and an outer continental shelf (OCS) State for receiving payments and contributions. The workshop also considered the framework, process and criteria for the equitable distribution by the Authority of payments and contributions. The recommendations of the Beijing Workshop are intended to form the basis for further consideration of the issues associated with the implementation of Article 82 by the relevant organs of the Authority in 2013 and beyond.

The Authority wishes to express its appreciation to CIMA and the Chinese Ministry of Foreign Affairs for their support and cooperation in holding the Beijing Workshop.

Michael W. Lodge
Deputy to the Secretary-General
and Legal Counsel
International Seabed Authority

Zhiguo Gao
Director
China Institute of Marine Affairs
Judge
International Tribunal for the Law of the Sea

---

1   In this report, we use the term 'Outer Continental Shelf', but acknowledge that others use the term 'Extended Continental Shelf'. In using the word 'Outer', we neither express nor imply any preference over the word 'Extended', but simply use it for consistency. There is only one continental shelf, defined under Article 76 of the Convention.

List of Terms and Abbreviations

Agreement, the	Model Article 82 Agreement
Area (the)	International Seabed Area
Authority (the)	International Seabed Authority
Beijing Workshop	International Workshop on Further Consideration of the Implementation of Article 82 of the United Nations Convention on the Law of the Sea, 26-30 November 2012, Beijing, China
Chatham House	Royal Institute for International Affairs of the United Kingdom
CIMA	China Institute for Marine Affairs
CLCS	Commission on the Limits of the Continental Shelf
Convention (the)	The United Nations Convention on the Law of the Sea
ECOSOC	United Nations Economic and Social Council
EEZ	Exclusive Economic Zone
Etopo5	World digital elevation model, generated from a digital database of land and sea-floor elevation on a 5-minute latitude/longitude grid, National Geophysical Data Center (NGDC), National Oceanic and Atmospheric Administration (NOAA)
Etopo2	Global digital elevation model, represents gridded (2 minute by 2 minute) elevation and bathymetry for the world, NGDC, NOAA
Etopo1	One arc-minute global relief model of earth's surface that integrates land topography and ocean bathymetry, NGDC, NOAA
GEBCO1	The GEBCO One Minute Grid, an ArcInfo Grid version (one arc-minute resolution) of the original data source gridone.grd NetCDF file, which is part of the GEBCO Digital Atlas Centenary Edition, Food and Agriculture Organization, United Nations
ISA	International Seabed Authority (also 'the Authority')
ITLOS	International Tribunal for the Law of the Sea
Landsat TM7	Landsat Enhanced Thematic Mapper 7, most recent satellite of Landsat mission launched on 15 April 1999
LDC	Least Developed Countries
LLS	Land-Locked States
LOSC	The United Nations Convention on the Law of the Sea
LTC	Legal and Technical Commission
OCS	Outer Continental Shelf
OCS State, the	A State that has an outer continental shelf
Pacific ACP States	Pacific African Caribbean Pacific States
SMS	Seafloor Massive Sulphides
SPLOS	States Parties to the Convention on the Law of the Sea
UNCITRAL	United Nations Commission on International Trade Law
UNCLOS III	Third United Nations Conference on the Law of the Sea, the
UNDP	United Nations Development Programme
VCLT 69	Vienna Convention on the Law of Treaties, 1969
VCLT 86	Vienna Convention on the Law of Treaties between States and International Organizations or between International Organizations, 1986

Opening and Welcoming Remarks at the Opening Session of the Workshop

Opening Remarks by Mr. Michael Lodge,
Deputy to the Secretary-General and Legal Counsel of the International Seabed Authority

Mr. Jia Guide, Deputy Director General of the Department of Treaty and Law, Ministry of Foreign Affairs of China; Dr. Haiwen Zhang, Deputy Director CIMA; H.E. Mr. Nii Allotey Odunton, Secretary-General of the International Seabed Authority; distinguished participants, colleagues and friends,

1. Good morning, and welcome to Beijing for the International Workshop on Further Consideration of the Implementation of Article 82 of the United Nations Convention on the Law of the Sea, which we are pleased to convene in collaboration with China Institute for Maritime Affairs (CIMA).

2. Some of us have had the pleasure of being in China for several days already, participating in the Third International Symposium on the Outer Continental Shelf and the Area. Others have just arrived over the weekend. I hope we have all had a good chance to relax and refresh, ready for the work over the next few days.

3. This workshop has been very long in the planning. We first began discussion of Article 82 in February 2009, when we convened a meeting of a small group of experts at Chatham House in London, in collaboration with the Royal Institute for International Affairs of the United Kingdom. That meeting, which was later referred to as the Chatham House Seminar, resulted in two publications, in the form of ISA technical studies, which I am sure many of you have read. These publications are also available for you today in your folders.

4. One of the recommendations of the Chatham House Seminar was to continue and broaden the discussion on the issues relating to the implementation of Article 82 by convening a further workshop involving representatives of key stakeholder groups, including members of the Legal and Technical Commission, representatives of member States, representatives of industry groups that may be affected by Article 82, technical experts and others.

5. This proposal was discussed by the Assembly of the ISA and it was agreed to include provision for a workshop in the work programme for the 2011-2013 period. Unfortunately, it was not possible to make immediate progress, mainly because the legal resources of the ISA were overwhelmed by the unexpected request by the Council to seek an Advisory Opinion from the Seabed Disputes Chamber, which meant that we were fully committed – both financially and in terms of human resources – throughout 2010 and the first half of 2011.

6. In 2011, however, during the Second International Symposium on the Continental Shelf, which took place in Hangzhou last year, a conversation took place with Judge Zhiguo Gao, Director of CIMA and a member of the International Tribunal for the Law of the Sea (ITLOS), in which we discussed the possibility of CIMA co-hosting the Article 82 workshop. Judge Gao had been one of the original participants in the Chatham House seminar, so it seemed a natural progression to move from London to Beijing to continue the discussion of Article 82 issues and to move from one prestigious research institution – Chatham House – to another.

7. We also decided to take advantage of the Third International Symposium on the Continental Shelf to convene this workshop back-to-back with the symposium. This allowed us to take advantage of the presence in Beijing of a number of experts who were attending the Third International Symposium, and in particular a number of members of the CLCS – we are delighted to welcome you to our meeting today.

8. Unfortunately, events are not always foreseeable. Despite the long and careful forward planning, we were taken by surprise a few days ago when ITLOS received an urgent claim for prompt release, requiring all the judges to immediately return to Hamburg for a hearing tomorrow. I know that Judge Gao, as well as Judges Golitsyn, Yanai and Park, were extremely disappointed to have to cancel their participation in this workshop, but we all understand that events took over and it was unavoidable.

9. Indeed, as members of the Law of the Sea community, we may perhaps look on the positive side and celebrate the fact that the Tribunal is so busy and is being so actively used by States Parties.

10. Despite his absence, I am pleased to say that Judge Gao played a full part in the preparations for this workshop and has graciously made available the full resources of CIMA. He remains a fully committed co-host in spirit if not in person. Not least, I am delighted that he has delegated Dr. Haiwen Zhang, Deputy Director of CIMA to represent him at this opening session.

11. Now I would like to give the floor to our distinguished speakers to formally open the workshop.

Welcome Remarks by H.E. Mr. Nii A. Odunton, Secretary-General of the International Seabed Authority

Distinguished Mr. Jia Guide, Deputy Director-General of the Department of Treaty and Law, Ministry of Foreign Affairs, Professor Haiwen Zhang, Deputy Director of CIMA, colleagues, ladies and gentlemen,

Good morning.

I wish to extend a warm welcome to you to this International Workshop on Further Consideration of the Implementation of Article 82 of the United Nations Convention on the Law of the Sea (the Convention), which is convened by the ISA in conjunction with China Institute for Marine Affairs (CIMA) of the State Oceanic Administration of China here in Beijing.

I am very impressed and encouraged to see such a nice turnout from about 23 member States of the ISA. As you may have noticed from the participants list, we have among us not only law professors, practicing lawyers, scientists and applied scientists from the private sector, but also senior government officials, legal advisors and diplomats, as well as current and former senior officials of international organizations including the United Nations, members of the United Nations Commission on Limits of the Continental Shelf, a Judge of the International Tribunal for the Law of the Sea, and members of the Legal and Technical Commission of the ISA.

As part of the overall legal regime for the continental shelf established under the Convention, Article 82 is an important component of the concept of the common heritage of mankind. Whilst Article 82 is clear in terms of its purpose, its language leaves a number of important practical issues unresolved. Much further work remains to be done if the provisions are to be applied uniformly and consistently in State practice. In order to avoid potential future disputes over the interpretation and application of Article 82, it is crucial that these issues are resolved as soon as possible. Clear guidance as to how Article 82 will be implemented in the future will also help to provide greater certainty to the marine minerals industry and enable it to promote more activities on the outer continental shelf (OCS).

Article 82, paragraph 4, stipulates that one of the responsibilities of the ISA under the scheme for payments and contributions with respect to the exploitation of the continental shelf beyond 200 nautical miles will be to distribute the payments and contributions to States Parties to the Convention, The ISA's work on resolution of the issues associated with the implementation of Article 82 commenced with the 2009 Chatham House seminar in London. As proposed in the Secretary-General's annual report to the Assembly during the sixteenth session of the ISA in 2010, this work is now included in the ISA's work programme for the period 2011-2013. Accordingly, and as a follow-up of the Chatham House seminar, the 2012 Beijing Workshop aims at drawing up guidelines for the implementation of Article 82 and of a model agreement between the ISA and an OCS State for receiving payments and contributions. The workshop will also consider the framework, process and criteria for the equitable distribution by the ISA of payments and contributions. The recommendations of the workshop will then form the basis for further consideration of the issues by the relevant organs of the ISA in 2013.

I wish to thank the Chinese Government for its firm support of the workshop, and all of you for your support by coming from all parts of the world to Beijing, and by contributing to the workshop with your expertise. I look forward to the results of your interactions during the next four and half days with confidence that the workshop will be a successful one.

Once again, thank you all very much.

Welcome Remarks by Mr. Jia Guide, Deputy Director-General of the Department of Treaty and Law, Ministry of Foreign Affairs of China

On the occasion of the opening of the International Workshop on Further Consideration of the the Implementation of Article 82 of the United Nations Convention on the Law of the Sea, I am honoured to extend, on behalf of the Department of Treaty and Law of the Chinese Foreign Ministry, warm congratulations to the workshop and a warm welcome to all the guests present today.

This year marks the 30th anniversary of the opening for signature of the United Nations Convention on the Law of the Sea. China and many other countries have held grand commemorative activities. It is true that some parts of the Convention are codification of custom international law, but it is also obvious that many provisions of the Convention reflect the new development of international law, which embodies the wisdom and hard work of our forerunners who created the Convention. Article 82 is definitely such a forward-looking and ground-breaking provision in the Convention. Our workshop is dedicated to the implementation of Article 82. Its mission is to go down the path guided by our forerunners and explore ways to flesh out the principles and ideas enshrined in the Convention. This is a unique way that we commemorate the Convention and pay tribute to our forerunners who gave birth to the Convention.

Since the advent of the Convention, Article 82 has been apparently dormant, and now many factors have made it timely to wake up the sleeping beauty. I will list a few: First, with the development of technology and economy, the prospect for coastal States to exploit non-living resources of their outer continental shelf is getting brighter. Second, the orderly operation of the International Seabed Authority, especially the adoption of three sets of regulations for exploration, fully testifies to the ISA's ability and experience, which are needed to elaborate rules, regulations and procedures concerning the implementation of Article 82 of the Convention. Third, being highly professional and efficient, the Commission on the Limits of the Continental Shelf has made recommendations on a number of submissions, thus providing a basis to finalize the outer limits of the continental shelf of coastal States. These elements combined laid a solid foundation for the international community to conduct substantive work on the implementation of Article 82 of the Convention.

When studying the implementation of Article 82 of the Convention, we are faced with good opportunities; however we should by no means underestimate the challenges. Article 82 is a complex and comprehensive Article that touches upon legal and political, economic and technical as well as many other issues. The implementation of Article 82 calls for a balanced approach to dealing with the interests of coastal States and the overall interests of the international community. Meanwhile, particular consideration should be given to the interests and needs of the developing States. When we study the implementation of Article 82, we should exercise caution and take a step-by-step approach. The result of our study should be strictly in compliance with the spirit of the Convention, and should also be able to withstand the test of history.

I would like to express my special thanks to the International Seabed Authority and the China Institute for Marine Affairs for co-hosting this workshop. This workshop provides a platform for communication and exchanges of views on the implementation of Article 82 of the Convention. I am pleased to note that renowned experts from various fields of work are present at the workshop, including scholars from universities and research institutes, officials from governments, representatives from academia and industry, representatives from the developing and the developed States, as well as members of the Legal and Technical Commission of the ISA, who will shoulder the responsibilities in drafting relevant regulations with respect to Article 82. It is our honour and privilege to have with us Honourable Mr. Satya Nandan, who participated in the negotiation and drafting of the Convention 30 years ago. As a witness to the birth of the Convention, he will provide valuable advice to our workshop. I am confident that with the joint efforts of everyone present, the workshop will achieve complete success!

Before I close, I would like to express my thanks to the ISA and Chatham House for holding a workshop in 2009 in London. The fruitful results from the London Workshop have laid a sound basis for us to carry forward in Beijing.

Finally, may I wish you all a happy stay in Beijing!

Welcome Remarks by Dr. Zhang Haiwen, Deputy Director, China Institute for Marine Affairs (CIMA), State Oceanic Administration

First of all, on behalf of CIMA and Prof. Zhiguo Gao, I'd like to extend my warmest welcome to all distinguished guests, new and old friends.

My sincere thanks go to ISA represented by Mr. Nii Odunton, for your trust in CIMA and inviting CIMA to co-organize this important workshop.

Last week, CIMA and the Second Institute of Oceanography co-organized the Third International Symposium on Scientific and Legal Aspects of the Regimes of the Continental Shelf and the Area. Many distinguished gentlemen seated on the podium and in the room attended the said Symposium. My team and myself are greatly honoured to have the opportunity to serve you again. Also, we are greatly honoured and are ready to provide local secretariat services to all participants, new and old friends.

Besides, we have made a special arrangement for all participants to pay a one-day visit to Tianjin, the third biggest city of China, to relax a little bit in the course of intense discussion at the workshop.

I wish all distinguished participants a pleasant stay in Beijing, and I also wish this workshop success!

Workshop Report

Background

1. Article 82 (Payments and contributions with respect to the exploitation of the continental shelf beyond 200 nautical miles) of the United Nations Convention on the Law of the Sea (the Convention) provides:

   1. The coastal State shall make payments or contributions in kind in respect of the exploitation of the non-living resources of the continental shelf beyond 200 nautical miles from the baselines from which the breadth of the territorial sea is measured.
   2. The payments and contributions shall be made annually with respect to all production at a site after the first five years of production at that site. For the sixth year, the rate of payment or contribution shall be 1 per cent of the value or volume of production at the site. The rate shall increase by 1 per cent for each subsequent year until the twelfth year and shall remain at 7 per cent thereafter. Production does not include resources used in connection with exploitation.
   3. A developing State which is a net importer of a mineral resource produced from its continental shelf is exempt from making such payments or contributions in respect of that mineral resource.
   4. The payments or contributions shall be made through the Authority, which shall distribute them to States Parties to this Convention, on the basis of equitable sharing criteria, taking into account the interests and needs of developing States, particularly the least developed and the land-locked among them.

2. As part of the overall legal regime for the continental shelf established under the Convention, Article 82 is an important component of the concept of the common heritage of mankind. Whilst the intent behind Article 82 is clear, its language leaves a number of important practical issues unresolved. Much further work remains to be done if the provisions are to be applied uniformly and consistently in State practice. In order to avoid potential future disputes over the interpretation and application of Article 82, it is important that these issues are resolved as soon as possible. Clear and unambiguous guidance as to how Article 82 will be implemented in the future will also help to provide greater certainty to the offshore industry and enable it to promote more activity on the outer continental shelf (OCS).

3. The ISA's work on resolution of the issues associated with the implementation of Article 82 commenced with a seminar convened by the ISA in conjunction with the Royal Institute of International Affairs (Chatham House) in London from 11 to 13 February 2009 (the Chatham House seminar). The Chatham House seminar was attended by a broad selection of leading academic and practitioner experts in the international law of the sea, marine geology and oceanography, as well as the offshore oil and gas industry from Europe, Africa, Asia, North and South America. As a result of this seminar, in 2009 and 2010, the ISA published two technical studies dealing with the legal and policy issues associated with the implementation of Article 82 (Technical Study No. 4) and the technical and resource issues associated with the OCS (Technical Study No. 5), respectively.

Sessions and Presentations

4. The International Workshop on Further Consideration of the Implementation of Article 82 of the United Nations Convention on the Law of the Sea, was held in Beijing, China, from 26 to 30 November 2012 (the Beijing Workshop), in collaboration with the China Institute for Marine Affairs of the State Oceanic Administration of China (CIMA).

5. The Beijing Workshop was attended by about 40 legal and scientific experts, including some current members of the Legal and Technical Commission (LTC) and the Commission on the Limits of the Continental Shelf (CLCS), senior experts from the offshore oil and gas industry, law firms, geosciences and natural resources research institutes, University law and marine science

professors, Foreign Ministry legal advisors and diplomats, former and current senior officials of the United Nations Division for Ocean Affairs and the Law of the Sea and the ISA. Participants were from the following member States of the ISA: Argentina, Australia, Brazil, Canada, China, Fiji, Germany, Ghana, Ireland, Japan, Mexico, Mozambique, Nigeria, Norway, Portugal, Slovenia, Tonga, Trinidad and Tobago, and the United Kingdom. A list of participants appears as Appendix 2 to the current report.

6. The workshop was practically oriented, aimed at producing draft proposals for consideration by OCS States and by the relevant organs of the ISA. It was informed by a number of background papers and informal working papers prepared and presented by experts and by a series of case studies of domestic licensing regimes and views on the implementation of Article 82 in selected OCS States. It's focus, however, was on the two working groups tasked with producing concrete proposals and recommendations.

7. A total of ten sessions were conducted during the workshop. A programme of the workshop appears as Appendix 1. On 26 November 2013, at the Opening Session, Mr. Michael Lodge, Deputy to the Secretary-General and Legal Counsel of the ISA briefed the participants on the preparation of the Beijing Workshop. Welcoming remarks were made by Mr. Nii A. Odunton, Secretary-General of the ISA, Mr. Jia Guide, Deputy Director General of the Department of Treaty and Law, Ministry of Foreign Affairs of China, and Dr. Haiwen Zhang, Deputy Director of CIMA.

8. The Opening Session was followed by Session 1: Setting the Scene, which was chaired by Mr. Michael Lodge. He introduced the participants, elaborated the workshop programme and outline, expected results and outcomes. He indicated that the Beijing Workshop should be by nature a working meeting with the later part dedicated to working group discussions. He emphasized that all participants, regardless of their national positions, were present at the Workshop in their personal capacities on the basis of their expertise, in order to stimulate a free and open discussion of all the issues. In this regard he proposed that the Chatham House Rule would apply to the Workshop, namely, non-attribution. Outcomes would be the product of the Workshop as a whole, and purely advisory based on expertise. With regard to expected outcomes of the Workshop, he suggested that participants bear in mind the following points:

    *   Submit a recommendation for consideration by the relevant organs of the ISA of guidelines for implementation of Article 82 of the Convention and a model agreement between OCS States members of the ISA and the ISA;
    *   The recommendations should be aimed at member States, the Council and the Assembly;
    *   Obligations under Article 82 (1) and Article 82 (2) are obligations of the OCS States parties to the Convention and the ISA's role is under Article 82(4) to receive and distribute payments;
    *   Ultimately, the Assembly is to approve rules, regulations and procedures for the equitable sharing of payments and contributions, acting on the recommendation of the Council in accordance with Art. 162(2)(o) of the Convention;
    *   The Council may refer all or some matters to the LTC or the Finance Committee for advice. Indeed, the 1994 Agreement makes it clear that any proposal having budgetary implications must be referred to the Finance Committee – should any aspect of the implementation of Article 82 be considered to have budgetary implications;
    *   It is not for the Council to instruct member States how to implement national responsibilities. However, the proposal for a model agreement would be an agreement among OCS States (as members of the ISA) and other members of the ISA as to modalities for implementation of this difficult article;
    *   The ultimate aim is a consensual understanding amongst States Parties for a consistent and uniform State practice in the implementation of Article 82.

9. Mr. Kening Zhang, Principal Legal Officer of the ISA, reviewed the outcome of the Chatham House seminar.

- Sessions 2 to 4 were dedicated to subjects including status of resources of the outer continental shelf, guidelines for the implementation of Article 82, possible options for equitable distribution of payments and contributions and settlement of disputes. These three sessions were respectively chaired by Dr. Kaiser de Souza, Chief, Division of Marine Geology, Geological Survey of Brazil, Ministry of Mines and Energy of Brazil and Member of the LTC; Mr. Michael Lodge, Deputy to the Secretary-General and Legal Counsel of the ISA; and H.E. Ambassador Eden Charles, Deputy Permanent Representative of Trinidad and Tobago to the United Nations, New York. During these three sessions the following presentations were made:
- Status of non-living resources of the OCS by Dr. Harald Brekke, Senior Geological and Project Coordinator, Norwegian Petroleum Directorates, Member of the LTC, and former member, Vice-Chairman and Acting Chairman of the CLCS;
    - Status of submissions to the CLCS and impacts of the submissions on the extent of the Area by Dr. Galo Carrera Hurtado, Honorary Consul of Mexico in Nova Scotia and New Brunswick, Canada, and Member of the CLCS;
    - Exploring the Extended Continental Shelf by Professor Clive Schofield, Director of Research and ARC Future Fellow, Australian National Centre for Ocean Resources and Security, University of Wollongong, Australia;
    - Introduction to the working paper on guidelines for the implementation of Article 82 and draft model agreement between ISA and OCS State by Professor Aldo Chircop, Marine and Environmental Law Institute, Schulich School of Law, Dalhousie University, Canada;
    - Canadian experience with regard to royalties from offshore oil and gas industry by Mr. Wylie Spicer, Q.C., Counsel, Norton Rose Canada LLP, Alberta, Canada;
    - Possible options for equitable distribution of payments and contributions by Professor Frida M. Armas-Pfirter, Austral University, Argentina; Member of the Finance Committee, ISA; and
    - Settlement of disputes arising from interpretation of the agreement between the ISA and an OCS State by Mr. Aleksander Čičerov, Minister Plenipotentiary, Ministry of Foreign Affairs, Slovenia, and Member of the LTC.

10. Sessions 5 to 7 were devoted to case studies of domestic licensing regimes and views on the implementation of Article 82. These three sessions were respectively chaired by Mr. Isaac Owusu Oduro, Chief Programme Officer, Programme Planning, Monitoring and Evaluation, Environmental Protection Agency of Ghana, and Member of the CLCS; Mr. Christopher Whomersley, Deputy Legal Adviser, Foreign & Commonwealth Office, the United Kingdom; and Ambassador Satya N. Nandan, former Secretary-General of the ISA. Presentations during these three sessions included:

- Brazil's practice and experience in its domestic licensing regimes and views on the implementation of article 82 with regard to its OCS oil and gas activities by Dr. Kaiser de Souza, Chief, Division of Marine Geology, Geological Survey of Brazil, Ministry of Mines and Energy; Member of the LTC, and Dr. Carlos Alberto Xavier Sanches, Deputy Manager of Government Participation, National Agency of Petroleum, Natural Gas and Biofuels - ANP – Brazil;
- The Brazilian oil and gas industry royalties by Dr. Carlos Alberto Xavier Sanches, Deputy Manager of Government Participation, National Agency of Petroleum, Natural Gas and Biofuels - ANP – Brazil;
- United Kingdom's practice and experience in its domestic licensing regimes and views on the implementation of article 82 with regard to its OCS oil and gas activities by Mr. Christopher Whomersley, Deputy Legal Adviser, Foreign & Commonwealth Office, the United Kingdom;
- Canada's continental shelf related practices and issues by Professor Ted McDorman, Legal Bureau, Department of Foreign Affairs and International Trade, Canada /University of Victoria;
- Norway's practice and experience in its domestic licensing regimes and views on the implementation of article 82 with regard to its outer continental shelf oil and gas activities by Dr. Harald Brekke, Senior Geological and Project Coordinator, Exploration Department,

Norwegian Petroleum Directorates; Member of the LTC, and former Member, Vice-Chairman and Acting Chairman of the CLCS;

- Portugal's practice and experience in its domestic licensing regimes and views on the implementation of article 82 with regard to its outer continental shelf oil and gas activities by Dr. Pedro Cardoso Madureira, Department of Geosciences, University of Evora, Portugal; Member of the LTC;
- Nigeria's practice and experience in its domestic licensing regimes and views on the implementation of article 82 with regard to its offshore oil and gas activities by Dr. Adesina Thompson Adegbie, Assistant Director, Nigerian Institute for Oceanography and Marine Research, Nigeria; Member of the LTC;
- Japan's practice and experience in its domestic licensing regimes with regard to its CS oil and gas activities and views on implementation of Article 82 by Mr. Tohru Furugohri, Principal Deputy Director of Ocean Division, International Legal Affairs Bureau, Ministry of Foreign Affairs, Japan;
- Status of Argentina's submission of OCS claim to the CLCS by Professor Frida Armas-Pfirter, Austral University, Argentina; and
- Ireland's practice and experience in its domestic licensing regimes and views on the implementation of Article 82 with regard to its OCS oil and gas activities by Mr. Declan Smyth, Deputy Legal Adviser, Department of Foreign Affairs & Trade, Ireland.

11. During these sessions on case studies, there were four parallel meetings of Working Group A (on implementation guidelines and Article 82 agreement), and Working Group B (on recommendations for equitable distribution of payments and contributions). The last two substantive sessions were given to plenaries, at which the Facilitators and Rapporteurs of the two Working Groups reported the outcomes of the group discussions, and reviews were conducted before the workshop was closed.

12. In addition to Article 82 and other relevant provisions of the Convention and Technical Study No. 4 of the ISA on issues associated with implementation of Article 82 of the Convention, the discussions by Working Group A on implementation guidelines and model Article 82 Agreement were facilitated by the informal working paper entitled Development of Guidelines for the Implementation of Article 82, contributed by Professor Aldo Chircop of the Marine and Environmental Law Institute, Schulich School of Law, Dalhousie University, Canada (See Annex 1 to this report).

13. The working paper recalls that the 2009 Chatham House seminar recommended that the anticipated relationship between an OCS State and the ISA should be governed by a novel bilateral international agreement. The Chatham House seminar also recommended that the ISA consider developing implementation guidelines and in particular taking the initiative to develop a 'Model Article 82 Agreement' to facilitate the administration of the relationship, in consultation with OCS States and other States Parties to the Convention. Accordingly, the working paper explores a possible framework for a Model Article 82 Agreement and identifies issues and questions for further discussion at the Beijing Workshop. The paper identifies considerations in the international law of treaties, especially with regard to agreements between States and international organizations that potentially assist the framing of the relationship.

14. The paper notes that while some of the gaps in Article 82 are essentially of an administrative nature and can be addressed in the Model Agreement, there are likely other substantive issues that may need to be referred to States Parties to the Convention on the Law of the Sea (SPLOS) for further guidance. The central focus of the working paper is a framework for the proposed Agreement. As suggested by the author of the working paper, the Model Agreement would include preambulatory and operative clauses. The latter would consist of clauses grouped under the following themes: use of terms and scope; Convention duties; provisions common to both payments and contributions in kind; provisions regarding payments; provisions regarding

contributions in kind; interruption or suspension of production; monitoring and confidentiality of data and information; interpretation and dispute settlement; and final provisions. In the paper several major questions are posed for discussion with regard to: identification of substantive issues which require guidance from States Parties of the Convention; usefulness of the framework Model Article 82 Agreement and how it can be improved; whether OCS States should be encouraged to opt only to make payments; how the ISA should take delivery of contributions in kind where an OCS State uses this option; potential monitoring role for the ISA; and approach to the settlement of disputes between OCS States and the ISA. The paper concludes by noting that the ISA should be expected to incur costs in the administration of Article 82 Agreements and invites workshop participants to consider how such costs might be recovered.

15. Session 8, on workshop outcomes, chaired by Mr. Michael Lodge, Deputy to the Secretary-General and Legal Counsel of the ISA, was held on the afternoon of 29 November and the morning of 30 November 2013. Facilitators and Rapporteurs of Working Groups A and B presented their respective oral reports on the outcomes of the discussions during the Workshop for consideration by the plenary. Participants commented and exchanged views on the two reports. Following the workshop, the Facilitators and Rapporteurs of the two Working Groups revised the reports to reflect the comments made and views expressed by participants during both the working group and the plenary deliberations. The reports of Working Groups A and B can be found in Annexes 1 and 2, respectively. Annex 3 gives a summary of the conclusions and recommendations of the Workshop.

Closing session

16. Following the session on outcomes of the Workshop, the review and closing session (Session 9) of the Beijing Workshop was conducted on 30 November 2012, under the co-chairmanship of Mr. Michael W. Lodge, Deputy to the Secretary-General and Legal Counsel of the ISA, and Dr. Haiwen Zhang, Deputy Director of CIMA.

17. In his closing remarks Mr. Nii A. Odunton, Secretary-General of the ISA, extended his gratitude to all the participants for their invaluable contributions and insights leading to the successful conclusion of the Workshop. He also, on behalf of all the participants and the ISA, expressed his appreciation for the tremendous support to the Workshop by CIMA and the Chinese Foreign Ministry. He informed participants that a report summing up the discussions and recommendations during the Workshop would be prepared by the Secretariat of the ISA along with the Facilitators and Rapporteurs of the two Working Groups for information and consideration of the relevant organs of the ISA in 2013, followed by publication of an ISA Technical Study containing all the documents prepared for, and presented at the Workshop.

18. Having joined the Secretary-General in thanking all the participants, Dr. Haiwen Zhang stated that China would continue to support ISA's endeavour with regard to the implementation of Article 82, and CIMA would further its study of the issues associated with the implementation of Article 82 so as to contribute more to this on-going task of the ISA.

Annexes

Annex 1

Report of Working Group A on Implementation Guidelines and Model Article 82 Agreement Presented by Professor Chircop as Facilitator, and Dr. Galo Carrera, Consulate of Mexico in Nova Scotia and New Brunswick, Canada, as Rapporteur

1. With Professor Chircop as its Facilitator, and Dr. Galo Carrera, Consulate of Mexico in Nova Scotia and New Brunswick (Canada) and member of the CLCS as its Rapporteur, Working Group A focused its deliberations on the following four major themes: (1) the nature of the relationship between the OCS States and the ISA for Article 82 purposes; (2) the terminology used in the provision; (3) explicit and implicit functions and tasks in the provision; and (4) possible options for structure and process to facilitate implementation. The Working Group's deliberations also resulted in (5) the recommendations presented at the end of the Workshop. These were reported upon by Professor Chircop and Dr. Carrera in turn as follows:

I. Relationship

2. Article 82 has relationships at two levels. At one level, mutual reciprocal duties among State Parties are created by virtue of subscription to the Convention, hence the trade-off between Article 76 (Definition of the continental shelf) and Article 82. Thus compliance with Article 82 is first and foremost an expectation of State Parties, i.e., the legal obligation to make payments or contributions in Article 82(1) is owed by the OCS State to other States Parties.

3. At another level, the procedure for compliance with Article 82 requires the OCS State to interact with the ISA. The latter is explained chiefly by the employment of the term "through" in Article 82(4). Clearly, the implementation of Article 82 requires a cooperative relationship between the OCS State and the ISA. That relationship must be guided by good faith. The ISA's role in that relationship must be interpreted in accordance with its mandate in the Convention. Working Group A emphasized the need to develop a cooperative relationship.

4. The Convention is silent on the precise point in time the relationship between the OCS State and the ISA emerged and what structure and process should govern it. In essence, the role of the ISA vis-à-vis the OCS State can be described as a 'receiver' rather than 'collector' of payments and contributions. The ISA then becomes a trustee of received amounts until they are distributed to beneficiaries in accordance with the Convention. While the ISA has not been expressly tasked by Article 82 or been conferred powers for monitoring and compliance, transparency in the implementation of Article 82 towards other State Parties is an important aspect of implementation. It was also pointed out that although the ISA has not been expressly granted a monitoring function, it would need certain data and information from the OCS State in order to be able to perform the role of receiver and eventually of channel of benefits to other State Parties.

5. Thus in order for the ISA to be in a position to receive payments and contributions and to further discharge downstream responsibilities, administrative procedures need to be established. In this regard, the working paper on 'Development of Guidelines for the Implementation of Article 82' provides guidance for some of the tasks that could potentially be part of such procedures. Clear procedures are needed to address gaps and ambiguities in Article 82 while at the same time providing for convenience, efficiency and transparency. Procedures should include various administrative tasks, such as notices to be provided by the OCS State to the ISA (e.g., regarding commencement, suspension and termination of production), notices provided by the ISA to the OCS State (e.g., currency of payments, bank account for payments, delivery of contributions in kind), and provision of information by the OCS State (e.g., regarding production and the basis for the computation of payments).

6. Working Group A explored the advantages and disadvantages of a standardized approach to making payments or contributions in contrast to a case-by-case approach. For example, there is

merit in encouraging OCS States to use commonly agreed procedures with the ISA in the interests of consistency, predictability and efficiency. A guide could be developed to assist OCS States for this purpose. At the same time, it was noted that different resources may require variable implementation and therefore there was equal merit in maintaining a measure of flexibility.

7. The information flow between the OCS State and the ISA was considered in depth. While the ISA is not answerable to member States for OCS States' discharge of their obligation under Article 82, and cannot be expected to comment on Article 82 compliance, its annual report will be expected to report on payments and contributions actually received or not received. This would be analogous to information provided on operators' certificates of expenditure with regard to activities in the Area. It is conceivable that the ISA's Secretary-General is queried by member States on various Article 82 matters, including the basis of computation of payments and amounts due. The provision of such information by the Secretary-General would clearly draw on notices and information voluntarily communicated to the ISA by the OCS State concerned.

8. To facilitate information flow and to assist with transparency, one possible approach is to recommend to OCS States that they consider a standardized format for presentation of information to accompany payments and contributions. The format could include the amounts and contributions in kind made, an explanation of how those amounts are arrived at and the sites concerned.

9. The discharge of the Article 82 obligation through contributions in kind raises several issues and challenges for the relationship between an OCS State and the ISA. When negotiated at the Third United Nations Conference on the Law of the Sea, 1973-1982 (UNCLOS III), the intention behind insertion of contributions in kind was to secure resource access to State Party beneficiaries. The exercise of this option gives rise to several difficulties. For example, it is unclear at what point in time legal title over the share of the resource composing the contribution in kind actually passes. Provision for transfer of title would need to be made to enable the resource to be distributed or marketed by the ISA. Logistical arrangements would need to be made and it is unclear who bears this responsibility and related costs, in particular where logistics require storage and transportation. Different resources would pose different challenges (e.g., marketing of natural gas, the price of which is determined by regional markets). The relationship between an OCS State and the ISA would likely require more onerous cooperation. The ISA does not have the capacity to receive contributions in kind and would effectively have to make appropriate brokerage and marketing arrangements. Costs would be incurred. Further, OCS States have the right to choose the option and there appears to be no restriction regarding possible change of discharge option. The complexity of implementation on the basis of contributions in kind is such that Working Group A reiterated the recommendation made at the 2009 Chatham House workshop, namely that OCS States should be encouraged to discharge the obligation solely on the basis of payments.

II. Terminology

10. Article 82 does not provide definitions for key terms used, in particular 'resource', 'all production', 'value', 'volume', 'site', 'payments', 'contributions in kind' and 'annually'. It is important to appreciate that these terms were employed in Article 82 in order to secure the compromise needed, functioning more as instruments of compromise than terms of art. Each term requires individual clarification, with reference to the use of other terms, to correctly and fairly reflect the intention behind the whole provision and in the context of the Convention. It was noted that in different OCS States some of these terms may not be understood in the same manner or might no longer be in use as a result of departure from royalty-based approaches to determine a government's share of produced resources to other forms of revenue-sharing (e.g., taxation). While a measure of flexibility of interpretation in particular cases might be desirable, the terms also represent common denominators for all OCS States for the implementation of Article 82. Therefore, reasonably consistent understanding among State Parties to facilitate implementation and avoid potential disputes regarding interpretation is an important

consideration. The development of a guide to assist OCS States with the implementation of Article 82 would need to address this matter.

11. The meaning of 'resource', while clearly referring to non-living resources, could have different meanings with regard to different resources in terms of what is effectively captured by Article 82 and at what point in time. For example, while on the one hand iron ore is exploited, on the other hand the purpose is a derived resource such as raw iron for the production of steel. The use of this term has a close relationship to 'production' and 'value' as it helps identify at what point production occurs and the value to be placed on the defined commodity at that time. A potential concern could be with regard to a produced resource that might not have market value until some processing occurs.

12. Article 82(2) refers to 'all production'. As with 'value', this could mean gross or net production. During negotiations of Article 82 at UNCLOS III the possibility of using the net was considered, but it was thought that it was simpler to consider the gross because of the diversity of accounting systems. The provision indicates what is excluded from the computation of production, namely that resources used in the exploitation of the resource are not to be included in calculating all production. However, clarification on this point is needed because a portion of the produced resource may be used for various purposes before marketing. For example, in the case of hydrocarbons such use of the resource may be for re-injection to enhance production, help stabilize a well, measure flow rates, generate energy on board the installation, and flaring. In the case of the analogy to the production of iron ore, it is possible that the ambiguity may extend to whether production refers to the iron ore or the derived commodity (e.g., raw iron). However, a cross-reference to the term 'site' (production at the site), assuming that 'site' is defined so as to refer to the actual point of extraction, may give rise to a meaning of the raw resource as and when produced at that location. The definition of 'volume' is closely related to production and raises similar issues.

13. The term 'value' is one of the more complex terms. It is capable of different meanings, in particular whether it refers to the gross or net value from production of the resource. The meaning could vary with reference to different resources (which are also commodities) and may further vary in tax and royalty regimes. It is a term that has a relationship to the meaning to be assigned to 'production'. When Article 82 was negotiated in the 1970s value was likely used with reference to production from relatively shallow wells in contrast to contemporary production and in particular in deep waters. In a contemporary context, deep water drilling has a particular cost structure and can be expected to exceed $200 million dollars per well. Moreover, it may not be possible to refer to a global valuation of a resource (e.g., as in the case of the price of oil and various minerals) where the practice is to value the resource according to a regional market (e.g., as in the case of natural gas). It was felt that whatever meaning assigned, it is essential that there be disclosure of the method of calculation in the interests of transparency, good faith and consistent application. Additional concerns with value arise where the price of a resource is artificial and when the currency used has an artificial or non-market-based value. These issues strengthen the argument for the use only of convertible currencies.

14. At UNCLOS III 'site' was understood in very simple terms. Site is potentially ambiguous as it could have several different meanings including a resource field, geological structure, well site, license area and a whole development area subject to multiple licenses. The technical term could be understood differently with regard to different resources. In relation to hydrocarbons, new wells to enhance resource recovery and multiple satellite wells drilled at different times over a long-term development could add complexity. A production site might also be restructured over the life of a field to enhance production. Further, if sites are defined with reference to very small areas of the same field, the resources of some sites could be exhausted in a short period, for example during the grace period. Defining 'site' can have additional complex dimensions in the case of a transboundary resource (straddling neighbouring outer continental shelves or an outer continental

shelf and the Area) that might require unitization and/or joint development. It is conceivable that production might take place on only one side of the maritime boundary. The most practical approach is likely to leave the determination of 'site' for Article 82 purposes to the OCS State, possibly with the assistance of guidelines.

15. 'Payments' was generally understood as monetary transfers. Article 82 does not prescribe a particular currency and in the absence of a common denomination it is conceivable that various currencies may be used depending on the originating OCS States. The international practice is for international payments (e.g., assessed contributions for membership in intergovernmental organizations, trust funds, and payments to the International Oil Pollution Compensation Fund) to be effected in an international currency or a widely used convertible currency, such as the US dollar, euro or other denomination. The US dollar is in current practice with regard to payments made to the ISA. Payments in different currencies could carry a potential risk of loss (or gain) in the amount transferred in fluctuating currency markets and likely conversion costs. Also, the prices of resources in commodity markets fluctuate, raising a question as to the relevant point in time to determine value for the purpose of effecting payment. A complicating factor is the possibility that the amount of payment (as it represents value) at the time received may be different from the amount at the time it is transmitted. For this and other reasons, it will be important for payments to be made within a reasonable time frame.

16. The difficulties to be encountered when an OCS State opts to make 'contributions in kind' have already been addressed in this report. In addition to those difficulties, an understanding of what is acceptable as a contribution in kind within the letter and spirit of the provision is necessary. Discussions in the Working Group proceeded on the assumption that this phrase refers to a share of the resource, but other possible interpretations were not discussed.

17. There is considerably less ambiguity in the term 'annually'. Different OCS States may have varying financial years. 'Annual' could also mean a calendar year commencing from the date of first production for a site. It was pointed out that different dates of commencement for different sites within the same jurisdiction could pose a potential complication for industry, which is likely to prefer a single definition to apply to all sites. In this respect, a first year of production could be prorated to the actual number of months of production, using a value based on average prices for the period covered. A definition should aim at simplicity and convenience.

18. Working Group A felt that a clear and common understanding of the terminology, and especially the functions performed by those terms in the contemporary context of Article 82, requires expert input into the discourse, which could be in the form of a study of the use of those terms in contemporary regulatory and industry practices across different jurisdictions. Some Working Group A participants felt that the responsibility for interpreting those terms ultimately lies with the OCS State, whereas others were of the view that an understanding of comparative practices would be useful. Such a study would help inform deliberations and would not be prescriptive in nature. A glossary of terminology would be useful. In the event that even after further study the issues raised still required authoritative interpretation, the matter may have to be referred to States Parties to the United Nations Convention on the Law of the Sea (SPLOS).

III. Functions and tasks

19. Apart from the making of payments or contributions by OCS States through the ISA, Article 82 contains no express text regarding specific tasks for the performance of States' obligations. However, as noted earlier in the report, the provision generates an administrative relationship between the OCS State and the ISA. There are certain functions that must be performed through specific tasks, some of which were identified in the Working Paper. In particular, information needs to flow through formal notice between OCS States and the ISA on various matters. Insofar as possible notices from OCS States to the ISA are concerned, the following were mentioned:

- That a particular site has become Article 82-eligible;
- Date of commencement of production;
- Suspension of grace period, including explanation;
- Suspension of production that affects payments or contributions, including explanation;
- Announcement of forthcoming payment, including explanation of how the amounts concerned were arrived at (payment to be made within a reasonable period following the end of the production year);
- Announcement of forthcoming contribution in kind and related arrangements, including explanation of how the amounts concerned were arrived at (deliveries, timeframes and related arrangements for contributions in kind would need to be made with the ISA);
- Announcement of change of option;
- Date of termination of production.

20. Insofar as likely notices from the ISA to the OCS State are concerned, the following were mentioned:

- Acknowledgement of receipt of all formal notices from the OCS State;
- Banking instructions regarding payments;
- Receipting of payment;
- Receipting of contribution in kind and related arrangements;
- Annual statement of account certifying received payments or contributions.

21. Further to the discussion on contributions in kind reported above, it was felt that where an OCS State opted to discharge its obligation in this manner, the contribution should be liquidated at the earliest opportunity, ideally at the point of production or reasonably soon thereafter. A brokerage service might be an efficient way to undertake this task. In any case, where an OCS State opts in this direction, it should give sufficient advance notice to the ISA bearing in mind the requirements of marketing. Expenses (e.g., brokerage) are likely to be incurred by the ISA. How these might be covered should be the subject of specific study. In a hypothetical scenario where an OCS State chooses to alter a prior exercised option, i.e., to change contributions in kind to payments or vice versa, specific advance notice should be given to the ISA, bearing in mind that the payment or contribution is to be made on an annual basis.

22. The annual report of the ISA's Secretary-General would inform Member States of payments and contributions received and related matters on the basis of information received from OCS States.

IV. Structure and process

23. A major theme addressed by Working Group A throughout its deliberations was what form of structure (formal or informal) and process would be needed to facilitate the administrative relationship between OCS States and the ISA. The Working Group generally felt that a 'do nothing' approach was not helpful or tenable. An implementation agreement similar to those for Part XI and straddling stocks and highly migratory species was considered highly undesirable. A model formal Article 82 agreement between OCS States and the ISA as proposed in the Working Paper was not considered appropriate or feasible, because of the limited mandate given to the ISA in Article 82 and its terms of reference. However, some elements discussed in the Working Paper, as long as they occur within the mandate of the ISA, were considered useful to consider in some other form. A memorandum of understanding between OCS States and the ISA was proposed, but not discussed in depth. Generally, the Working Group preferred a different option, namely a voluntary 'guidance document', which would provide helpful guidelines for all OCS States.

24. By and large, the content of the guidance document should be a practical instrument that would capture much of what has been presented in this report, in particular: terminological matters; format for certification and explanations to accompany the methodology used for determining amounts of payments and contributions; notices that could be provided to the ISA;

and information and notices expected in return. The document would, in essence, be advisory in character and would assist OCS States in the discharge of the obligation in a transparent manner. One suggestion was to encourage OCS States to undertake an annual audit of the payments or contributions in accordance with public sector auditing standards and requirements. This would further strengthen transparency. The document would need to take into consideration the needs of different resource scenarios. The document must not embark on an independent interpretation of Article 82, as this is a responsibility of State Parties to the Convention. The ISA would take the lead in preparing the guidance document in accordance with its own internal structures and procedures. The Authority has significant experience in bringing appropriate expertise to assist with the development of a document of this type.

V. Recommendations

25. Working Group A felt that the initiative to facilitate the pragmatic and functional implementation of Article 82 should continue to be taken by the ISA. Despite the intensive discussions in the Working Group, it was felt that some issues could not be covered (e.g., dispute settlement) or did not receive sufficiently thorough and informed consideration. Clearly, further intensive deliberations are called for. To assist with the next steps, the Working Group produced the following conclusions and recommendations:

- The ISA should encourage OCS States, in particular those that are issuing or plan to issue offshore licences for the exploitation of the non-living resources of the outer continental shelf, to consider and anticipate the implementation needs of Article 82 within their respective jurisdictions.
- OCS States, while enjoying the exclusive choice to make payments or contributions in kind, should be encouraged to opt only for payments in the interests of simplicity and efficiency of implementation. It is conceivable that a SPLOS resolution may be needed to move this recommendation forward.
- As discussed in this report, further examination of the implementation needs of Article 82 would benefit from a study of key terms as they are used in contemporary regulatory and industry practices across different jurisdictions. The study should consider various hydrocarbons and mineral resource scenarios. As an information document, the study would help identify possible paths for a practical approach. The study would help build and deepen understanding of the terminological issues in realistic settings, but would not have prescriptive value.
- The ISA should explore further the concept of a Memorandum of Understanding between an OCS State and the ISA, or a guidance document, and take steps to prepare a draft for discussion, bearing in mind that such instruments will be essentially voluntary and aim to provide practical guidelines and advice to assist OCS States in the implementation of Article 82. The content should reflect terminological matters, functions and tasks, and other appropriate implementation matters discussed in this report. It could be undertaken in three sections, namely: (a) practical and administrative arrangements; (b) provisions regarding contributions in kind; and (c) considerations for OCS States to take into account.

Annex 2

Report of Working Group B on Recommendations for Equitable Distribution of Payments and Contributions, Presented by H.E. Ambassador Eden Charles, Deputy Permanent Representative of Trinidad and Tobago to the United Nations, New York, as Facilitator, and Mr. Kenneth Wong, Counsellor (Commercial), Embassy of Canada in Beijing as the Rapporteur

1. The mandate of Working Group B was to submit recommendations for equitable distribution of payments and contributions under Article 82 paragraph 4 of the Convention. H.E. Ambassador Eden Charles, Deputy Permanent Representative of Trinidad and Tobago to the United Nations, New York, served as Facilitator, and Mr. Kenneth Wong, Counsellor (Commercial), Embassy of Canada in Beijing, served as the Rapporteur. The deliberations of Working Group B were reported by Ambassador Charles and Mr. Wong as follows:

2. Article 82(4) provides: "The payments or contributions shall be made through the ISA, which shall distribute them to States Parties to this Convention, on the basis of equitable sharing criteria, taking into account the interests and needs of developing States, particularly the least developed and the land-locked among them."

3. Working Group B started with a textual analysis of key terms in Article 82(4), from which suggestions for consideration can be inferred. It submitted that the term 'through' must not be interpreted to mean 'to' the ISA because it views the ISA as a conduit for transmissions of payments and contributions to States Parties in accordance with 82(1). In this regard, the role of the ISA is only instrumental. The final destination of the payments and contributions is the States Parties. In seeking to interpret 'through the Authority', the Group observed that the following should be taken into consideration:

   • The need for the ISA to establish a mechanism for collecting payments and contributions and then distributing them in a timely and efficient manner to States Parties.
   • The establishment of this mechanism may entail additional costs for the ISA. Consequently this could be done through possibly: the regular budget of the ISA; or
   • the ISA retaining an agreed percentage of the amounts collected to cover the associated costs.
   • Possible role for the Finance Committee – Perhaps there is a possible role for the Finance Committee to recommend what would be a reasonable percentage for the ISA to retain to cover administrative costs. It was also argued that the Convention does not contemplate such a function for the Finance Committee and as a result, the Council of the ISA would have to mandate the Finance Committee to assume this task.
   • It was also felt that the ISA should redistribute the payments and contributions in a timely and efficient manner.
   • The Working Group also advanced that there would be no need for the ISA to establish a fund for the purposes of investing the payments and contributions received from States Parties because this would be inconsistent with the objective of timely and efficient distribution.

   I. Beneficiaries under Article 82(4)

4. For the purpose of 82(4), the Working Group submits that in order to determine what constitute States Parties, the following definition in Article 1(2)(1) of the Convention should be used, namely, '"States Parties" means States which have consented to be bound by this Convention and for which this Convention is in force.'

   • In this regard, the Working Group distinguished between the provisions of Article 140, which governs activities in the Area that are for the benefit of mankind as a whole from those of Article 82 which covers the resources of the Outer Continental Shelf (OCS).

- Notwithstanding the mention of other entities under Articles 160(2)(f)(i) and 162(2)(o)(i) the beneficiaries of the payments and contributions of the OCS could only be States Parties as this is specifically determined under Article 82(4).
- Accordingly, Articles 160 and 162, which refer to the functions of the Assembly and the Council respectively, mention both the equitable sharing of financial and other economic benefits derived from activities in the Area (defined in Article 140) as well as the equitable sharing of payments and contributions made pursuant to Article 82, however without changing the specific definitions of beneficiaries under Articles 82 and 140, respectively.

II. Equitable Sharing Criteria

5. In seeking to determine what constitute equitable sharing criteria under Article 82(4), it was argued that the ISA would need to develop and maintain a set of criteria to be used to calculate amounts to be distributed to all States Parties. It should be recalled that under article 162(2)(o)(i), the Council is charged with the responsibility to recommend to the Assembly rules, regulations and procedures on the equitable sharing of the payments and contributions made pursuant to Article 82.

6. In determining equitable sharing criteria, the ISA is bound to take into account "the interests and needs of developing States, particularly the least developed and the land-locked among them".

7. It was agreed that, based on the wording of 82(4), the eight States Parties that are both Land-Locked States (LLS) and Least Developed Countries (LDC) would have the highest priority and the highest ranking. The 37 State Parties that are either LLS or LDC would be next, and then other similar categories may be considered, such as Small Island Developing States and Geographically Disadvantaged States. These would be followed by other developing States Parties, and then the remainder of the States Parties. To assist in ranking and in determining quantitative scores for the States Parties, the ISA may consider using the following: the UN scale of assessed contributions adjusted to take into consideration the number of States Parties to the Convention; the United Nations Development Programme (UNDP) Human Development Index; and other indices or lists that may be found relevant for this purpose.

8. Regarding 'interests and needs', there was some discussion as to whether the use of the Assessed Contributions list and Human Development Index as a proxy for quantifying 'needs' was sufficient. No effective way to more fully account for 'interests and needs' could be enunciated however.

9. A literal interpretation of 82(4) provides that the payments and contributions should go directly to the States Parties. Article 82(4) however also indicates that "interests and needs of developing States" must be taken into account. For this purpose it was suggested that in keeping with the object and purpose of the Convention, it may be possible to distribute the payments and contributions through established programmes and funds to help developing States meet their targets under, for example, the Millennium Development Goals.

10. In order to discharge the responsibility of distributing and properly accounting for 'equitable sharing criteria', the ISA would need to develop and maintain a list with quantitative values to be used to calculate amounts to be distributed to States Parties. This list should be updated as new data becomes available, e.g. the United Nations Economic and Social Council evaluates the LDC list every three years, and the UNDP Human Development Index is issued annually.

Annex 3

Summary of Conclusions and Recommendations of the Workshop

1. As indicated in paragraph 4 of the Report of the Beijing Workshop, the Workshop was particularly intended to be tasked with, firstly, drawing up recommendations for Article 82 implementation guidelines and the outline of a model Article 82 agreement between the ISA and an OCS State for receiving payments and contributions, and secondly, considering the framework, process and criteria for the equitable distribution by the ISA of payments and contributions. The recommendations of the expert group meeting were then expected to form the basis for further consideration of the issues by the relevant organs of the ISA. Extensive exchanges of views were conducted at the Workshop among participants in Working Group A on implementation guidelines and a model Article 82 agreement and Working Group B on equitable distribution of payments and contributions. Based on the reports of the two Working Groups submitted by the Facilitators and Rapporteurs and notes taken by the Secretariat of the Workshop, a summary of conclusions and recommendations of the Workshop has been prepared as follows:

2. The initiative to facilitate the pragmatic and functional implementation of Article 82 should continue to be discussed through the relevant organs of the ISA. Despite the intensive discussions during the Beijing Workshop, some issues such as dispute settlement could not be covered or did not receive sufficiently thorough and informed consideration. Further intensive study and deliberations are required.

3. The ISA should encourage OCS States, in particular those that are issuing or plan to issue offshore licences for non-living resources of the outer continental shelf, to consider and anticipate the implementation needs of Article 82 within their respective jurisdictions.

4. OCS States, while enjoying the exclusive choice to make payments or contributions in kind, should be encouraged to opt to make payments in the interests of simplicity and efficiency of implementation. It is conceivable that a resolution by the States Parties to the Convention may be needed to move this recommendation forward.

5. Further examination of the implementation needs of Article 82 would benefit from a study of key terms discussed in this report as they are used in contemporary regulatory and industry practices across different jurisdictions. The study should consider various hydrocarbons and mineral resource scenarios. As an information document, the study would help identify possible paths for a practical approach. The study would help build and deepen understanding of the terminological issues in realistic settings, but would not have prescriptive value.

6. The ISA should explore further the concept of a Memorandum of Understanding between an OCS State and the ISA, or a guidance document, and take steps to prepare a draft for discussion, bearing in mind that such instruments will be essentially voluntary and aim to provide practical guidelines and advice to assist OCS States in the implementation of Article 82. The content should reflect terminological matters, functions and tasks, and other appropriate implementation matters discussed in this report. It could be undertaken in three sections, namely: (a) practical and administrative arrangements; (b) provisions regarding contributions in kind; and (c) considerations for OCS States to take into account.

7. Article 82(4) provides: "The payments or contributions shall be made through the Authority, which shall distribute them to States Parties to this Convention, on the basis of equitable sharing criteria, taking into account the interests and needs of developing States, particularly the least developed and the land-locked among them." The Workshop considered that the term 'through' must not be interpreted to mean 'to' the ISA because it views the ISA as a conduit for transmissions of payments and contributions in kind to States Parties in accordance with Article 82(1). In this regard, the role of the ISA is only instrumental. The final destination of the

payments and contributions is the States Parties. In seeking to interpret "through the Authority", the Workshop observed that the following should be taken into consideration:

- The need for the ISA to establish a mechanism for collecting payments and contributions and then distributing them in a timely and efficient manner to States Parties.
- The establishment of this mechanism may entail additional costs for the ISA. Consequently this could be done through possibly: the regular budget of the ISA or, the ISA retaining an agreed percentage of the amounts collected to cover the associated administration costs.
- Possible role for the Finance Committee – Perhaps there is a role for the Finance Committee to recommend what would be a reasonable percentage for the ISA to retain to cover administrative costs. It was also argued that the Convention does not contemplate such a function for the Finance Committee and as a result, the Assembly or Council of the ISA would have to mandate the Finance Committee to assume this task.
- It was also felt that the ISA should redistribute the payments and contributions in a timely and efficient manner.
- Some participants felt that there would therefore be no need for the ISA to establish a fund for the purposes of investing payments and contributions received from States Parties because this would be inconsistent with the objective of timely and efficient distribution.

8. In seeking to determine what constitutes equitable sharing criteria under Article 82(4), it was suggested that the ISA would need to develop and maintain a set of criteria to be used to calculate amounts to be distributed to all States Parties. It is recalled that under article 162(2)(o)(i) of the Convention, the Council is charged with the responsibility to recommend to the Assembly rules, regulations and procedures on the equitable sharing of the payments and contributions made pursuant to Article 82.

9. In determining equitable sharing criteria, the ISA is bound to take into account "the interests and needs of developing States, particularly the least developed and the land-locked among them." It was suggested that, based on the wording of 82(4), the eight States Parties that are both Land-Locked States (LLS) and Least Developed Countries (LDC) would have the highest priority and the highest ranking. The 37 State Parties that are either LLS or LDC would be the next, and then other similar categories may be considered, such as Small Island Developing States) and Geographically Disadvantaged States. These would be followed by other developing States Parties, and then the remainder of the States Parties. To assist in ranking and in determining quantitative scores for the States Parties, the ISA may consider using the following: the UN scale of assessed contributions adjusted to take into consideration the number of States Parties to the Convention; the UNDP Human Development Index; and other indices or lists that may be found relevant for this purpose.

10. In order to discharge the responsibility of distributing and properly accounting for 'equitable sharing criteria', the ISA would need to develop and maintain a list with quantitative values to be used to calculate amounts to be distributed to States Parties. This list should be updated as new data becomes available, as in the case of ECOSOC, which evaluates the LDC list every three years, and that of UNDP, which issues its Human Development Index annually. It was suggested that the Secretariat of the ISA prepare a study or a trial list on the issue.

11. While Article 82(4) could be literally interpreted as to provide that the payments and contributions in kind should go directly to the States Parties, Article 82(4) however also indicates that "interests and needs of developing States" must be taken into account. For this purpose it was suggested that in keeping with the object and purpose of the Convention, it may be possible to distribute the payments and contributions in kind through established programmes and funds to help developing States meet their targets under, for example, the Millennium Development Goals.

Working Paper on Development of Guidelines for Implementation of Article 82 by Professor Aldo Chircop, Marine and Environmental Law Institute, Schulich School of Law, Dalhousie University, Canada

DEVELOPMENT OF GUIDELINES FOR THE IMPLEMENTATION OF ARTICLE 82

WORKING PAPER

Aldo Chircop

Marine & Environmental Law Institute

Schulich School of Law, Dalhousie University

Halifax, NS, Canada

Prepared for the International Workshop on Further Consideration of the Implementation of Article 82 of the United Nations Convention on the Law of the Sea, 1982, Beijing, 26-30 November 2012

October 2012

TABLE OF CONTENTS

Executive summary

This document is an issues paper concerning the implementation of Article 82 of the United Nations Convention on the Law of the Sea, 1982 (LOS Convention). It was commissioned by the International Seabed Authority (ISA) to assist discussion at an international workshop in Beijing in November 2012.

Article 82 contains a duty on States to make payments or contributions in kind with regard to production from non-living resources of the outer continental shelf (OCS), i.e., areas beyond the 200-nautical mile limit and up to the seaward limits of the continental shelf defined according to Article 76. A relationship is created between States having this obligation (OCS States) and the ISA as the institution tasked with receiving payments and contributions for distribution to other States Parties. The LOS Convention provides little guidance on the implementation of Article 82 by OCS States and the ISA.

At an international seminar at Chatham House, London, in 2009, it was recommended that the anticipated relationship between an OCS State and the ISA should be governed by a novel bilateral international agreement. It was further recommended that the ISA consider developing implementation guidelines and in particular to take the initiative to develop a 'Model Article 82 Agreement' to facilitate the administration of the relationship in consultation with OCS States and other States Parties to the LOS Convention.

This Working Paper explores a possible framework for a Model Article 82 Agreement and identifies issues and questions for further discussion at the Beijing workshop. The paper identifies considerations in the international law of treaties, especially with regard to agreements between States and international organizations that potentially assist the framing of the relationship. The paper notes that while some of the gaps in Article 82 are essentially of an administrative nature and can be addressed in the Agreement, there are likely other substantive issues that may need to be referred to States Parties to the United Nations Convention on the Law of the Sea (SPLOS) for further guidance.

The central focus of the Working Paper is a framework for the proposed Agreement. It would include preambulatory and operative clauses. The latter would consist of clauses grouped under the following themes: use of terms and scope; Convention duties; provisions common to both payments and contributions in kind; provisions regarding payments; provisions regarding contributions in kind; interruption or suspension of production; monitoring and confidentiality of data and information; interpretation and dispute settlement; and final provisions.

Several major questions are posed for discussion with regard to: identification of substantive issues which require guidance from SPLOS; usefulness of the framework Model Article 82 Agreement and how it can be improved; whether OCS States should be encouraged to opt only to make payments; how the ISA should take delivery of contributions in kind where an OCS State uses this option; potential monitoring role for the ISA; and approach to the settlement of disputes between OCS States and the ISA. The paper concludes by noting that the ISA should be expected to incur costs in the administration of Article 82 Agreements and invites workshop participants to consider how such costs might be recovered.

LIST OF TABLES

ACRONYMS AND ABBREVIATIONS

Agreement, the	Model Article 82 Agreement discussed in this Working Paper
Area, the	International Seabed Area
EEZ	Exclusive economic zone
ITLOS	International Tribunal for the Law of the Sea
LOS Convention	United Nations Convention on the Law of the Sea, 1982
OCS	Outer continental shelf (continental shelf areas beyond the 200-nautical mile limit and up to the outer of the continental margin as defined by Article 76)
OCS State, the	A State that has an outer continental shelf
SPLOS	States Parties to the United Nations Convention on the Law of the Sea, 1982
UNCITRAL	United Nations Commission on International Trade Law
UNCLOS III	Third United Nations Conference on the Law of the Sea, 1973-1982
VCLT 69	Vienna Convention on the Law of Treaties, 1969
VCLT 86	Vienna Convention on the Law of Treaties between States and International Organizations or between International Organizations, 1986

1. INTRODUCTION

The purpose of this Working Paper is to invite discussion on how Article 82 (Table 1) of the United Nations Convention on the Law of the Sea, 1982 (LOS Convention)[1] might be implemented. It builds on two earlier technical studies published by the International Seabed Authority (ISA), in particular a study on the legal aspects of the implementation of Article 82.[2] The Working Paper has been prepared as an 'issues paper' to serve as a background document for the International Workshop on the Implementation of Article 82 of the United Nations Convention on the Law of the Sea, to be held in Beijing, China, on 25-30 November 2012.

Table 1: Article 82

> Payments and contributions with respect to the exploitation of the continental shelf beyond 200 nautical miles
>
> 1. The coastal State shall make payments or contributions in kind in respect of the exploitation of the non-living resources of the continental shelf beyond 200 nautical miles from the baselines from which the breadth of the territorial sea is measured.
>
> 2. The payments and contributions shall be made annually with respect to all production at a site after the first five years of production at that site. For the sixth year, the rate of payment or contribution shall be 1 per cent of the value or volume of production at the site. The rate shall increase by 1 per cent for each subsequent year until the twelfth year and shall remain at 7 per cent thereafter. Production does not include resources used in connection with exploitation.
>
> 3. A developing State which is a net importer of a mineral resource produced from its continental shelf is exempt from making such payments or contributions in respect of that mineral resource.
>
> 4. The payments or contributions shall be made through the ISA, which shall distribute them to States Parties to this Convention, on the basis of equitable sharing criteria, taking into account the interests and needs of developing States, particularly the least developed and the land-locked among them.

---

1   United Nations Convention on the Law of the Sea, Montego Bay, 10 December 1982, UN Doc. A/CONF.62/122, 7 October 1982, online: http://treaties.un.org/doc/Publication/UNTS/Volume%201833/volume-1833-A-31363-English.pdf.

2   International Seabed Authority, Issues Associated with the Implementation of Article 82 of the United Nations Convention on the Law of the Sea, Technical Study No. 4 (Kingston: ISA, 2009), online: http://www.isa.org.jm/files/documents/EN/Pubs/Article82.pdf [hereafter Technical Study No. 4]; International Seabed Authority, Non-Living Resources of the Continental Shelf Beyond 200 Nautical Miles: Speculations on the Implementation of Article 82 of the United Nations Convention on the Law of the Sea, Technical Study No. 5 (Kingston: ISA, 2010), online: http://www.isa.org.jm/files/documents/EN/Pubs/TechStudy5.pdf. For scholarly treatment of the implementation issues of Article 82 see: Aldo Chircop, "Operationalizing Article 82 of the United Nations Convention on the Law of the Sea: A New Role for the International Seabed Authority?" 18 Ocean Yb 395-412 (2004); Michael W. Lodge, "The International Seabed Authority and Article 82 of the United Nations Convention on the Law of the Sea", 21(3) Int. J. Mar. & Coast. L. 323-333 (2006).

Table 2: Template of Article 82

Nature of rule	Rule	Elements
Basic rule	The OCS State shall make payments or contributions in kind in respect of the exploitation of non-living resources of the OCS.	OCS State has a choice between making (1) payments or (2) contributions in kind.
		Payments and contributions relate to non-living resources.
		Payments and contributions relate to exploitation leading to production.
Collateral rules concerning payments or contributions in kind.	Payments or contributions shall be made annually.	Payments or contributions shall be made regularly on an annual basis.
	Payments or contributions shall be made with respect to all production.	Payments and contributions are to be based on all production.
		Payments and contributions shall be calculated on the value or volume of production.
		Production does not include resources used in connection with exploitation.
	Payments or contributions commence on the sixth year of production and are based on a pre-set scale.	Grace period: obligation to make payments or contributions does not apply to the first five years of production.
		Pre-set scale: payments and contributions commence on the sixth year of production, on a scale starting at 1% of production in the sixth year and increasing by 1% per year until it reaches 7% in the twelfth year, which thereafter shall remain the ceiling.
Collateral rule concerning eligibility to make payments and contributions.	Net importing OCS developing States are exempted from making payments or contributions.	Exemption for OCS developing States: if a developing OCS State imports more of the resource subject to payments or contributions than it exports, it is exempted from the obligation in relation to that resource.
Collateral rule concerning distribution of benefits.	Payments and contributions are to be made through the ISA, which shall distribute them to States Parties.	Payments or contributions are to be made through the ISA.
		Beneficiary States: the ISA will distribute payments and contributions to States Parties on the basis of equitable sharing criteria, taking into account the interests and needs of developing States, especially the least developed and land-locked States.

Source: International Seabed Authority, Issues Associated with the Implementation of Article 82 of the United Nations Convention on the Law of the Sea, Technical Study No. 4 (Kingston: ISA, 2009), 27-28.

Although it is an integral part of the package deal in the LOS Convention, Article 82 has remained largely dormant because to date the anticipated conditions to bring it into effect have not materialized. The general scheme of the provision is set out in Table 2. Article 82 introduces an obligation on States enjoying outer continental shelves (OCS States) to make specified payments or contributions with regard to production from non-living resources of their continental shelves outside the 200-nautical mile limit, i.e., the outer continental shelf (OCS).[3] The payments and contributions are to be made through the ISA for eventual distribution to other State Parties in accordance with the

---

3   Note that not all producing OCS States will have this obligation. LOS Convention, supra note 1, Art. 83(3).

Convention. The key anticipated condition that will trigger the obligation is occurrence of production.

The provision essentially consists of a basic rule (i.e., the duty to make payments or contributions) and a series of collateral rules designed to give further substance and process to the basic duty. Even taking into consideration the basic and collateral rules, the Convention is largely silent on how Article 82 is to be implemented. What is clear is that qualifying OCS States and the ISA are assigned responsibilities for its implementation.

This Working Paper is an initial attempt at exploring how OCS States and the ISA might approach the task of implementation. While both OCS States and the ISA are assigned individual responsibilities, the performance of aspects of their respective responsibilities necessitates interaction and coordination between them.

The focus of the Working Paper is on aspects of Article 82 where the responsibilities of OCS States and the ISA meet and interact. The paper explores possible structure and process to assist that interaction. Article 82 is unprecedented and therefore there is little substantive practice to guide implementation.[4] Hence the working paper poses questions for discussion in exploring possible directions for implementation, including the development of guidelines.

The Working Paper builds on a novel idea and key recommendation made at the Seminar on Issues Associated with the Implementation of Article 82 of the United Nations Convention on the Law of the Sea, convened at Chatham House, London, on 11–13 February 2009, as follows:

> Given the likely long-term relationship between producing OCS States and the ISA, as well as the uncertainties identified in this report, it is advisable for a producing OCS State and the ISA to enter into an Article 82 agreement. For this purpose, and in anticipation of the operationalization of Article 82, it is advisable that the OCS States and the ISA formulate a 'Model Article 82 Agreement', within the framework of the LOS Convention, and upon which ISA/OCS State-specific agreements would be entered into in the future. Such an agreement would perform the function of an OCS royalty agreement and be the basis upon which the respective responsibilities in Article 82 (insofar as the making and handling of payments and contributions are concerned) can be coordinated and administered. It is advisable for the ISA to take the lead in developing such a model agreement, in close cooperation with experts from OCS States and other States Parties of the LOS Convention.[5]

The principal purpose of this Working Paper is to further develop the concept of a 'Model Article 82 Agreement' as an administrative framework and tool for the implementation of those aspects of Article 82 that concern the making of payments and contributions in kind by the OCS State and the ISA's responsibilities in receiving them.

2. BACKGROUND

Articles 82 and 76 were closely inter-linked during negotiations at the Third United Nations Conference on the Law of the Sea, 1973-1981 (UNCLOS III). The Declaration of Principles Governing the Sea-Bed and the Ocean Floor, and the Subsoil thereof, beyond the Limits of National Jurisdiction, 1970 declared that the seabed and subsoil beyond national jurisdiction was the common heritage of mankind and that no State could appropriate it. Areas beyond national jurisdiction would be developed in the interests of mankind and the ensuing benefits would be shared by all States, taking into particular consideration the interests and needs of developing countries.[6]

---

4   The only practice to date is the United States' with regard to Stipulation 10 inserted in leases in the Gulf of Mexico. This practice concerns additional domestic royalty to be levied if the United States becomes a party to the Convention. Although the practice might provide guidance for the domestic implementation of Article 82, it falls short of guiding the administrative aspects of a relationship between an OCS State and the Authority. Moreover, the United States is not a party to the Convention. See Technical Study No. 4, supra note 2, at 5-8.

5   Technical Study No. 4, ibid., at xvii-xviii.

6   UN General Assembly Resolution 2749, (XXV), 17 December 1970, UN Doc. A/RES/25/2749, 12 December 1970, online: http://www.un-documents.net/a25r2749.htm.

During UNCLOS III coastal States were successful in arguing for new and extensive maritime zones, in particular the 200 nautical mile exclusive economic zone (EEZ) and the OCS. Specifically with regard to the OCS, the more the outer limit was moved seawards, the more this occurred at the expense of the extent of the international seabed area. Many States, especially those that were land-locked and geographically disadvantaged, objected to encroachments on the Area. Towards the final stages of the Conference a compromise was needed to ensure broad support for Article 76 and achieve consensus on the final package deal. Article 82 was a key element in the trade-off. A finalized Article 76 introduced rules and a procedure for the definition of the outer limits of the OCS, accompanied by the duty to deposit a copy of charts showing the geographical coordinates of the outer limits of the OCS to the ISA.[7] Article 82 applied to any future production of non-living resources of the OCS and provided for the distribution of benefits to other State Parties and beneficiaries designated by the Convention, such as developing States, especially the least developed and land-locked States. The ISA was charged with the central role, and responsibility, of receiving the payments and contributions established by Article 82 and of developing equitable criteria for the distribution of those benefits.

In addition to providing rules and procedure for the definition of the outer limits of the continental shelf and thereby ascertain the full extent of coastal State sovereign rights and jurisdiction, a consequence of Article 76 is used to identify candidate continental shelf areas for Article 82 purposes. At the time of preparation of the Working Paper, there were 61 submissions to the Commission on the Limits of the Continental Shelf (CLCS) submitted in accordance with Article 76.[8] An additional 45 communications to the CLCS provided preliminary information.[9]

Both OCS States and the ISA need to consider how Article 82 will affect them. The OCS States making submissions to the CLCS need to be aware of the implications of this provision. At this time very few coastal States possessing an OCS have granted exploration and discovery licences to offshore operators. No production licences appear to have been issued. However, recent offshore deep water activity suggests that the expectation of resource discoveries holding promise for commercial production on the OCS is realistic.

As the institution charged by the Convention to receive payments and contributions and distribute these to designated beneficiaries, the ISA has substantial responsibilities to discharge. They require advance planning and preparation. For example, the ISA needs to set up structures and processes to enable it to receive payments and contributions in kind. The latter consists of a share of the produced resource. At this time, the ISA does not have the capacity to perform such tasks. It has not developed policies, rules and procedures to guide it in interacting with OCS States with regard to Article 82. Further, because the ISA is responsible for receiving payments and contributions from OCS States and for distribution of these benefits to States Parties to the Convention, it has as yet to develop criteria for distribution. The LOS Convention requires the ISA to develop rules, regulations and procedures in this regard. The Council, the executive organ of the ISA, is tasked with the recommendation of rules, regulations and procedures to the Assembly for the distribution of benefits on an equitable basis.[10] The Legal and Technical Commission (LTC) is the likely body that will develop regulatory proposals for the Council. The Assembly is the organ that ultimately considers and approves rules, regulations and

---

7   LOS Convention, supra note 1, Art. 84(2).

8   Several States made more than one individual or joint submission for different OCS areas. Division for Ocean Affairs and the Law of the Sea, online: http://www.un.org/Depts/los/clcs_new/commission_submissions.htm.

9   Numerous States, especially developing States, were unable to make submissions within the stipulated 10-year deadline from when the Convention entered into force in their regard. A Meeting of States Parties to the Convention decided that, pending the making of formal submission, provision of preliminary information on their expected OCS submission would have the effect of meeting the deadline requirement. See: Meeting of States Parties, SPLOS/183, 24 June 2008, Decision regarding the workload of the CLCS and the ability of States, particularly developing States, to fulfil the requirements of article 4 of Annex II to the Convention, as well as the decision contained in SPLOS/72, paragraph (a), online: http://www.un.org/Depts/los/meeting_states_parties/documents/splos_183e_advance.pdf; and SPLOS/72, 29 May 2001, Decision regarding the date of commencement of the ten-year period for making submissions to the CLCS set out in article 4 of Annex II to the United Nations Convention on the Law of the Sea, online: http://daccess-dds-ny.un.org/doc/UNDOC/GEN/N01/387/64/PDF/N0138764.pdf?OpenElement.

10   LOS Convention, supra note 1, Art. 162(2)(o)(i).

procedures recommended by the Council. Once adopted, they become rules of the ISA.[11] These tasks can be expected to take time because there will need to be consultations not only with OCS States but also more generally with States Parties to the LOS Convention.

3. RELATIONSHIP BETWEEN OCS STATES AND THE INTERNATIONAL SEABED AUTHORITY

Article 82 anticipates interaction between OCS States and the ISA. The interaction appears to be primarily of an administrative nature: the ISA receives payments and contributions from OCS States. The Convention is silent on the structure and process of this relationship. The only other text in the Convention which implies a process in the implementation of Article 82 is internal to the ISA, i.e., with reference to the recommendation and adoption of rules, regulations and procedures for the equitable sharing of payments and contributions.

In Technical Study No. 4 the implementation of Article 82 is envisaged in three phases.[12] The first phase is described as a 'pre-production period' covering the "prospecting, exploration and development licences or leases, but before commencement of commercial production." During this period there is no performance of responsibilities assigned to OCS States and the ISA. However, this period provides an opportunity for OCS States to anticipate the future obligation to make payments and contributions. Similarly, the ISA is in a position to prepare for the future discharge of its responsibilities by designing the procedures necessary to perform its mandate.

The second phase launches with the commencement of actual production and covers the first five-year production period. This represents the 'grace period' provided in Article 82. Technically, Article 82 becomes effective in this period in the sense that the Convention provides a notional count-down to maturity.

The third phase commences on the sixth year of production and represents the period when the duty to effect payments and contributions matures. This phase is described as the "OCS royalty period". commencing with the sixth year of production. This period will see annual royalty rate increments of 1 per cent until the ceiling of 7per cent is reached on the 12th year and will remain at that level for the remaining period of production.

This conceptualization of phases is useful to better locate and time implementation tasks and ultimately situate the proposed Model Article 82 Agreement. This approach provides the missing structure and process to the relationship between the OCS State and ISA. It is intended to be of assistance to OCS States and the ISA.

It is suggested that Phase I is an ideal period for commencement of planning for future implementation, .since there is not yet the pressure to deliver on legal obligations under the explicit timeframe in Article 82, thus providing time for consultation and reflection in developing a pragmatic and functional approach.

4. GENERAL CONSIDERATIONS REGARDING A MODEL ARTICLE 82 AGREEMENT

The ISA, in consultation with OCS States, is well positioned to lead the development of a Model Article 82 Agreement. It will be a party to all the bilateral agreements to be concluded as new OCS areas commence production.

---

11   LOS Convention, ibid., Art, 160(2)(f)(i). The Vienna Convention defines rules of an intergovernmental organization to mean "in particular, the constituent instruments, decisions and resolutions adopted in accordance with them, and established practice of the organization." Vienna Convention on the Law of Treaties between States and International Organizations or between International Organizations, Vienna, 21 March 1986 (not in force), United Nations Treaty Collection, http://untreaty.un.org/ilc/texts/instruments/english/conventions/1_2_1986.pdf [hereafter VCLT 86], Art. 2(1)(j). For a general discussion of the VCLT 86 see Karl Zemanek, "The Vienna Convention on Treaties between States and International organizations or between International Organizations," United Nations Audiovisual Library of International Law, 2009, online: http://untreaty.un.org/cod/avl/pdf/ha/vclt/vclt-e.pdf. For a more general work on issues concerning international organizations, see José E. Alvarez, "International Organizations: Then and Now," 100 Am. J. Int'l L. 324-347 (2006).

12   Technical Study No. 4, supra note 2, 46-47.

The purpose of the proposed Agreement is to facilitate implementation of the interrelated administrative responsibilities of the OCS State and ISA through a 'contractual approach'. The ISA already engages in contractual arrangements with contractors with regard to exploration and deep seabed mining in the Area. The OCS State and the ISA would also address on a bilateral basis the administrative and procedural uncertainties in the LOS Convention regarding how their respective responsibilities are to be performed. It is conceivable that there might be substantive issues concerning the interpretation and application of the LOS Convention, e.g., questions of a legal nature that speak to the rights and responsibilities of States. Where such issues are identified in the process of developing guidelines for the implementation and the Model Article 82 Agreement, they might have to be referred to a meeting of States Parties to the United Nations Convention on the Law on the Sea (SPLOS). If States Parties consider substantive interpretation issues to require a higher degree of formal agreement, there are precedents that would support this approach but which would likely require an extended diplomatic process.[13]

The proposed Agreement is not advanced as a 'one size fits all'. It is likely that each administrative relationship between the ISA and a different OCS State will have particular characteristics because of the OCS State's election to make payments or contributions in kind and the consequences that will flow from that decision. For example, if payments are made they potentially could be effected in different currencies, banking arrangements will differ and so on. In the case of contributions in kind the ISA will need to make arrangements for receiving the share of the produced resource. These realities argue for an approach to the development of the Model Article 82 Agreement that takes into consideration the need for: (a) common core provisions for all agreements; and (b) particular provisions for each agreement. The core provisions would ensure overall consistency and fairness. Some core provisions would naturally be adapted to each State Party. The particular provisions, on the other hand, would properly address the uniqueness of the requirements of implementation in each case.

The Agreement would not address matters of a purely domestic nature with regard to the production from the resource and instead the focus would be exclusively on those aspects of production that are central to the respective responsibilities in Article 82.

The legal status of an agreement between an OCS State and the ISA is that of a treaty between a sovereign State and an intergovernmental organization. As such, it will have specific features which, while informed by general principles of treaty law, will also have particular characteristics.[14] Among the unique characteristics are the engagement of the legal personality of an international organization in accordance with its constitutive instrument,[15] the development of an agreement involving the international organization that will be replicated or adapted to different State Parties, the giving of content to interrelated responsibilities established in a multilateral treaty, and an agreement which involves a Sovereign State as a Party in one capacity (as an OCS State) while at the same time being a member of the organization in another capacity (as LOS Convention State Party).[16]

The treaty relationship to be developed will be informed and guided by two key and à propos multilateral instruments: the Vienna Convention on the Law of Treaties, 1969 (VCLT 69), and the Vienna Convention on the Law of Treaties between States and International Organizations and

---

13   Namely: (1) Agreement relating to the Implementation of Part XI of the United Nations Convention on the Law of the Sea of 10 December 1982, New York, 28 July 1994, UN Doc. A/RES/48/263, 17 August 1994, online: http://daccessdds.un.org/doc/UNDOC/GEN/ N94/332/98/PDF/N9433298.pdf?OpenElement; (2) Agreement for the Implementation of the Provisions of the United Nations Convention on the Law of the Sea of 10 December 1982 relating to the Conservation and Management of Straddling Fish Stocks and Highly Migratory Fish Stocks, New York, 4 December 1995, UN Doc. A/CONF.164/37, 8 September 1995, online: http://www.un.org/depts/los/convention_ agreements/texts/fish_stocks_agreement/CONF164_37.htm [hereafter Straddling Stocks Agreement].

14   The preamble of the VCLT 86 noted that such agreements have specific features of treaties which involve international organizations as a different type of subject of international law than States. VCLT 86, supra note 11, preamble.

15   The preamble reiterates "the practice of international organizations in concluding treaties with States or between themselves should be in accordance with their constituent instruments." VCLT 86, ibid. In the Peace Treaties Case (2nd Phase), the International Court of Justice held that "such a clause was to be strictly construed and could be applied only in the case expressly provided hereby." The clause concerned the Secretary-General's power to appoint a tribunal member in a dispute settlement clause in a treaty between States. Advisory Opinion Concerning the Interpretation of Peace Treaties with Bulgaria, Hungary and Romania (Second Phase), 18 July 1950, I.C.J. Reports 1950, p. 221, online: http://www.unhcr.org/refworld/docid/4023a1fa2.html.

16   The preamble provides that "nothing in the present Convention should be interpreted as affecting those relations between an international organization and its members which are regulated by the rules of the organization." VCLT 86, supra note 11.

between International Organizations, 1986 (VCLT 86). The VCLT 69 is in force and widely regarded as having codified the general international law of treaties.[17] Although the VCLT 69 was conceived with inter-State treaty relationships in mind, it does not exclude application of principles to States Parties in regard to treaties that also have an international organization as a party.[18] It is unlikely that the proposed Agreement falls directly within the ambit of the VCLT 69, but in any case the very similar, if not identical, principles of the VCLT 86 are relevant to the Agreement.[19]

Potential concerns to consider in regard to the VCLT 86 are that: (a) the Convention is not yet in force; (b) many OCS States are not parties; and (c) the ISA is not a party. Technical Study No. 4 recommended that the ISA consider becoming a party.[20] The VCLT 86 was mandated by the UN General Assembly and was consciously developed by the International Law Commission to track closely the VCLT 69. Gaja writes that "it is likely that at least the substantive rules which were drafted on the basis of the model of the 1969 Convention will increasingly be considered as equivalent to rules of general international law."[21] The close relationship between the two Conventions clearly reflects unity of the treaty law regime.[22]

Several key treaty law principles will guide the development and implementation of the Agreement. The Agreement will be guided by the principle of good faith in its development and performance.[23] It will have a close relationship to the LOS Convention because it can be construed as a step in the performance of an obligation in the LOS Convention.[24] Considered on its own merits apart from the LOS Convention, the negotiation (or adaptation of the Model Article 82 Agreement to a given OCS State) will be governed by the good faith principle.[25] A party may not invoke an internal rule for the failure to perform a treaty obligation.[26] The Agreement would be subject to the principle of non-retroactivity.[27]

Issues of interpretation should be expected to arise. The interpretation of the Agreement would be similarly guided by the treaty law principle of interpretation in good faith and in light of context, object and purpose.[28] The object and purpose are to assist implementation of the LOS Convention obligations of the parties. The context of the purpose is clearly the LOS Convention.[29] The LOS Convention consists of a package deal that includes a trade-off between Articles 76 and 82 reflecting the rationale behind the making of payments and contributions. It is conceivable that during the performance of the OCS Agreement, the OCS State and the ISA may amend or enter into subsidiary agreements or develop a practice with regard to the implementation of the Agreement. In these cases the interpretation of the OCS Agreement would take those factors into consideration.[30] The development of the Model Article 82 Agreement and its adaptation to particular OCS States will

---

17   Giorgio Gaja, "A 'New' Vienna Convention on Treaties between States and International organizations or between International Organizations: A Critical Commentary," 58 B.Y.I.L. 253-269 (1987), 255.

18   Art. 3: "the fact that the present Convention does not apply to international agreements concluded between States and other subjects of international law ... shall not affect ... (c) the application of the Convention to the relations of States as between themselves under international agreements to which other subjects of international law are also parties." Vienna Convention on the Law of Treaties, Vienna, 23 May 1969, 1155 [hereafter VCLT 69]. U.N.T.S. 331 (in force: 27 January 1980).

19   VCLT 86, supra note 11, Art. 3.

20   Through accession under Art. 84, VCLT 86, ibid.

21   Gaja, supra note 17, at 269.

22   Gaja, ibid., 255.

23   VCLT 86, supra note 11, Art. 26.

24   LOS Convention, supra note 1, Art. 300. The duty includes an obligation to exercise rights that would not constitute "an abuse of right."

25   Tariq Hassan, "Good Faith in Treaty Interpretation," 21 Va. J. Int'l L. 443-481 (1980-1981), 451. Hassan finds further support for this contention in the work of Cheng, McNair, Schwarzenberger and Wolff.

26   VCLT 86, supra note 11, Art. 27.

27   VCLT 86, ibid., Art. 28: "Unless a different intention appears from the treaty or is otherwise established, its provisions do not bind a party in relation to any act or fact which took place or any situation which ceased to exist before the date of the entry into force of the treaty with respect to that party." An interesting consideration could arise with regard to OCS States embark on production from OCS resources prior to becoming parties to the LOS Convention. There could be an issue as to when Article 82 commences to operate with regard to such States. To remove potential uncertainty, the Model Agreement might need to expressly apply retroactively.

28   VCLT 86, ibid., Art. 31. A recent leading text on treaty interpretation to provide guidance on these issues is Richard K. Gardiner, Treaty Interpretation (New York: Oxford University Press, 2008).

29   VCLT 86, supra note 11, Art. 31(2): "The context for the purpose of the interpretation of a treaty shall comprise, in addition to the text, including its preamble and annexes: (a) any agreement relating to the treaty which was made between all the parties in connection with the conclusion of the treaty ..."

30   VCLT 86, ibid., Art. 31(3).

also be guided by supplementary means of interpretation.[31] Supplementary sources to support the Agreement in the implementation of Article 82 are likely to be useful because of the gaps and textual ambiguities in Article 82.

5. FRAMEWORK FOR A MODEL ARTICLE 82 AGREEMENT

5.1   Preambulatory Clauses

A preamble in the Agreement would be useful to provide context and rationale and would have value for interpretation purposes.[32] The preamble could include the following invocations by "The Parties to the Agreement":

- Recalling the context and purpose of the LOS Convention;
- Noting the existence and purpose of Article 82;
- Noting further that the OCS State and the ISA are assigned responsibilities for the purposes of the provision;
- Recognizing that the provision does not set out administrative procedures for the discharge of the responsibilities of the OCS State and the ISA; and
- Being mindful in concluding the Agreement of the need for each Party to develop an administrative framework and procedures to facilitate the implementation of Article 82.

5.2   Operative Clauses

I. Use of Terms and Scope

The Agreement will require an interpretation clause for (1) concepts and phrases considered or used as terms of art and (2) for the purpose of delimiting the scope of application of the instrument.

1.   Interpretation

For example:

'Authority': the International Seabed Authority.

'Contribution in kind': meaning a percentage share of the produced resource in accordance with the scale of assessment in Article 82(2).

'Convention': the United Nations Convention on the Law of the Sea, 1982.

'Outer continental shelf': to refer to the seabed and subsoil of the submarine areas beyond the limits of the EEZ of the OCS State and up to the outer limit of the continental shelf as defined in accordance with Article 76 of the Convention. This definition needs to track the text of Article 76.

'Payments': to refer to monies transferred to the ISA for the purposes of the discharge of the obligation.

'Production': to refer to all production of the resource other than any test production and produced resources used in connection with exploitation. This definition has to take into consideration Article 82(2) which qualifies eligible production so as to focus on commercial production. It takes into consideration that 'test production' is not 'commercial production;. It also takes into consideration that a part of the resource, such as gas, may be re-injected into a well to enhance production. It is conceivable that 'commercial production' might require further definition, possibly with reference to

---

31   VCLT 86, ibid., Art. 32: "Recourse may be had to supplementary means of interpretation, including the preparatory work of the treaty and the circumstances of its conclusion, in order to confirm the meaning resulting from the application of article 31, or to determine the meaning when the interpretation according to article 31: (a) leaves the meaning ambiguous or obscure; or (b) leads to a result which is manifestly absurd or unreasonable."

32   The context for the purpose of interpretation of a treaty includes the preamble and annexes. VCLT 86, ibid., Art. 31(2).

marketability of the produced resource or readiness for processing on a sustained basis.[33]

'Resource(s)': to refer to non-living resource(s) of the outer continental shelf.

'Site': to refer to the geographical location of a resource. The definition should ensure that site means the delineated field of the discovered resource, thereby avoiding an interpretation of site that refers to each individual point of extraction, e.g., per well.

'Value': to refer to the monetary value of the produced resource at the well-head in the case of hydrocarbons and extraction in the case of other non-living resources. The history of negotiations at UNCLOS III suggests that this was the meaning intended for value.

'Volume': to refer to the gross production of the produced resource, but excluding test production and production of resources used in connection with exploitation. This definition would need to be consistent with the Article 82(2) reference to 'all production'.

II. Convention Duties

2. Duty of the OCS State

The first substantive provision could reproduce the obligation of the OCS State in a manner that tracks the text of the LOS Convention, for example: 'The [name of OCS State] shall make payments or contributions in kind in respect of the production from the exploitation of the non-living resources of the outer continental shelf pursuant to Article 82 of the Convention and in accordance with the procedure set out in this Agreement.'

The provision should also state that the ISA is the institution responsible for receiving the payments and contributions and shall receive them in accordance with the procedure set out in this Agreement.

3. Notice to be provided to the ISA regarding choice of making payments or contributions in kind

The Convention provides the OCS State with the options of discharging the obligation by making payments or contributions in kind. The OCS State enjoys exclusive decision-making regarding the two options. In any case, the OCS State should give the ISA notice of its choice of option. The Agreement could address the choice in one of two ways.

- First, the notice of the option could be in the Agreement itself. This provides for simplicity and economy by focusing on one procedure for the discharge.
- Second, and in the alternative, the Agreement can include a provision that enables the OCS State to provide notice of the option at a later stage, but not later than by the end of the fifth year of production (i.e., end of the grace period). If this alternative is preferred the Agreement will need to include procedures for both payments and contributions as discussed below.

An interesting question is whether the Agreement should also provide for an OCS State to change the manner of discharge of the obligation and whether this should be anticipated in the text or can be left to future amendment of the Agreement. Ideally, and in the interest of simplicity, OCS States should be encouraged to commit to one option for the entire production life of a site.

III. Provisions Common to both Payments and Contributions in Kind

4. Grace period

Depending on the date of commencement of the Agreement (i.e., whether on start of production at the beginning of Phase II or on termination of the grace period and commencement of Phase III; see 'provision 21' below), a provision regarding the grace period is desirable. The first five years of commercial production are established by the Convention as a period that is free of payments

---

33   In the oil and gas industry a "commercial field" is defined as "[A]n oil and/or gas field judged to be capable of producing enough net income to make it worth developing." Oil & Gas UK, online: http://www.oilandgasuk.co.uk/glossary.cfm.

and contributions. The Agreement should address how this period is to be determined, including commencement and termination dates. If this is not determined in the Agreement, there will still need to be a separate agreement between the OCS State and the ISA regarding the formal commencement of the sixth year of production.

Although the LOS Convention is silent on the possibility of suspension of the grace period, the very intention behind the grace period is to enable the OCS State (or developer) to recover its development costs. Given that interruption of production will affect recovery of development costs within the allocated time frame, it is reasonable to interpret the five-year grace period not as a fixed period, but rather as a 'time account' for the benefit of the OCS State. If this is a reasonable and practical interpretation, there should be provision for the OCS State to give notice of interruption to the ISA at the earliest practicable opportunity. The interruption must be such as to justify suspension of the grace period, followed by eventual notice of resumption of production and revival of the remaining grace period. The OCS State should provide the ISA with an explanation of the circumstances that give rise to interruption of production and failure to do so should not result in interruption of the grace period.

5. Notice of commencement of production to the ISA

Technical Study No. 4 noted that the OCS State should be expected to give notice to the ISA of the impending application of Article 82.[34] This is not a stated requirement in Article 82 but can be characterised as an administrative matter related to the obligation to make payments or contributions. The OCS State is fully aware of the commencement date of commercial production and is therefore in a position to anticipate the date of commencement of the grace period (or Phase III). The notice should be at least 12 months before the obligation to make the first annual payment or contribution matures and will need to be a formal communication to the ISA.

The notice should contain technical information indicated or implied in Article 82 to enable full implementation of the provision, such as: identification of the producing site; official date of commencement of commercial production and consequent commencement of the grace period; type of non-living resource; value of production; and volume of eligible production.

6. Determination of amounts of payments and contributions in kind

The OCS State determines the amount of payments or contributions in kind due on an annual basis. The coastal State is best able to determine production amounts and consequently the determination of the amounts due is a logical corollary of that responsibility. The rates set out in the Convention should be re-stated in the Agreement (Table 3: Scale of Payments and Contributions).

The OCS State, through an authority designated by it in the Agreement, should certify that the amounts calculated, according to percentage of value in the case of payments and according to percentage of volume in the case of contributions in kind, are correct and in compliance with Article 82(2).

Table 3: Scale of Payments and Contributions

Production year	Scale in terms of % of value or volume
Years 1 to 5	0
Year 6	1
Year 7	2
Year 8	3
Year 9	4
Year 10	5
Year 11	6
Year 12 and subsequent years	7

---

34   Technical Study No. 4, supra note 2, 51.

Source: International Seabed Authority, Issues Associated with the Implementation of Article 82 of the United Nations Convention on the Law of the Sea, Technical Study No. 4 (Kingston: ISA, 2009), 35.

Given that it is the responsibility of the ISA on behalf of all State Parties of the Convention to receive the amounts due, Technical Study No. 4 argued that it is reasonable for the ISA to expect information and explanations of how the amounts due are arrived at. Such explanations would add a measure of transparency to the discharge of the obligation. This should be reflected in the Agreement.

7. Calculation of amounts due

The basis for computing the amounts due is 'all production'. This will need to be interpreted. One possible interpretation is 'commercial production', i.e., excluding test production, and that resources used in exploiting the resource are not to be included in the computation of production (e.g., natural gas re-injected to enhance recovery or to generate energy on board the installation, in the case of hydrocarbons). Flared gas may also have to be excluded as it is not produced for commercial purposes. Other expenses incurred in producing the amounts due may not be deducted because the purpose of the grace period is precisely to enable the OCS State (or developer) recover those costs.

It is reasonable to interpret the levy on 'all production' as implying that no local taxes and charges be levied against the payments and contributions in kind, as these would have the effect of reducing the amounts imposed in the legal obligation.

Subject to Provision 11 below, it is conceivable the OCS State provides services not reasonably implied in Article 82 (e.g., lengthy storage and transportation of contributions in kind). If this is anticipated, the OCS State and the ISA should include express provision on how to cover the expenses of actual services rendered and with the prior consent of the ISA.

8. Scheme of payments and contributions in kind

Payments and contributions in kind are due on an annual basis. 'Annual' will need to be defined by specifying actual date(s). By the end of a given production year the OCS State will have had to complete all payments/contributions due for that year. Specific dates would need to be set out. This will provide precision to the determination that a particular payment or contribution is in default or simply late.

There is nothing in Article 82 to prevent an interpretation that while discharging the obligation on an annual basis, the parties agree to a scheme of transfers spread throughout the year (e.g., quarterly, monthly or some other scheme). This could be a practical consideration where the OCS State opts to make contributions in kind. Multiple transfers in a given year would ostensibly be necessary to reduce storage costs.

A provision regarding 'time is of the essence' is desirable to avoid delays.

IV. Provisions regarding payments

9. Making of payments

Technical Study No. 4 proposed that where the OCS State opts to make payments it should make them in an international or convertible currency. The most common practice is the use of a national currency that is convertible and in widespread use. This is normal in the determination of national assessed contributions for memberships in international organizations.[35] An alternative but also common practice in international agreements is the utilisation of Special Drawing Rights (SDRs) as

---

35   E.g., contributions by UN Member States to the UN budget are computed in US dollars. See UN Secretariat, Assessment of Member States' contributions to the United Nations regular budget for 2012, UN Doc. ST/ADM/SER.B/853, 27 December 2011, online: http://www.un.org/ga/search/view_doc.asp?symbol=ST/ADM/SER.B/853.

a neutral measure which allows converstion to different currencies.[36] What is important is the receipt of payments in a currency that will enable the ISA to distribute them to other State Parties of the LOS Convention.

The Agreement should make provision for receipts to be issued by the ISA. By issuing receipts for amounts received, the ISA acknowledges sums received on account in discharge of the obligation. A useful addition could be for the ISA to issue an annual receipt and statement of accounts certifying amounts received in compliance with Article 82. In turn, the ISA would need to report compliance to its membership in its annual report on payments and contributions received.

The Agreement should anticipate the establishment of an account for each OCS State to enable payments to be made on account.

The OCS Agreement should specify the name of the contact institution in the OCS State that will be responsible for making payments and the counterpoint contact in the ISA. Details with regard to the manner, procedure and bank account should be included, possibly in an annex.

V. Provisions regarding Contributions in Kind

While this Working Paper reiterates the recommendation in Technical Study No. 4 that OCS States consider discharging the obligation solely through payments, the exercise of the option to make payments or contributions is clearly a decision exclusive to the OCS State. Accordingly, the application of provisions on the making and administration of contributions in kind in this section depends on the option exercised.

10. Making of contributions in kind

The central provision will address how the OCS State will compute the amount of contribution in kind due as a percentage of the volume of eligible production. The basis of production will need to be stated. The percentage will need to be calculated on the volume of 'all production' less the portion of the resource used in exploitation. No other deductions are permitted, nor may taxes or other charges be levied, as explained earlier.

As in the case of payments, the Agreement should make provision for receipts to be issued for contributions received on account by the ISA in discharge of the obligation. As mentioned elsewhere contributions can be expected to be received in allotments as the resource is produced, rather than in one annual allotment. Hence there will be a need for the ISA to issue an annual receipt and statement of account.

Again, as in the case of payments option, the OCS Agreement should specify the name of the contact institution in the OCS State that will be responsible for making contributions in kind and the counterpoint contact in the ISA or delegated institution. It is conceivable that the ISA may contract out the receiving of contributions in kind to a private commercial institution.

11. Delivery of contributions in kind

Where the OCS State opts to make contributions in kind the Agreement will need to anticipate the times (including frequency), location(s) and manner in which the ISA is to take delivery of the amounts due. If the ISA takes delivery, it will need to be in a position to do so without delay.

The Convention is unclear as to where the contribution in kind is to be made, i.e., whether on-site as produced or at the end of the transportation chain of the resource. The latter will likely involve costs for the OCS State.

---

36 For example the following conventions and their amending protocols: Convention on Limitation of Liability for Maritime Claims, London, 19 November 1976, 1456 U.N.T.S. 221; International Convention on Civil Liability for Oil Pollution Damage, London, 29 November 1969, 973 U.N.T.S. 3; International Convention on the Establishment of an International Fund for Compensation for Oil Pollution Damage, 18 December 1971, 1110 U.N.T.S. 57.

A possible approach is for the OCS State and the ISA to agree that the OCS State would arrange for delivery as instructed by the ISA. Should this be considered part of the Article 82 obligation, or should it be considered a service over and above the OCS State's obligations, the costs of which ought to be covered from another source? The Workshop is invited to consider this question.

12. Marketing of contributions in kind

Instead of taking delivery, the OCS State and ISA might agree on marketing the contribution in kind on the open market with the assistance of the OCS State as soon as possible. A variation is to provide the OCS State with an option to buy the resource. The Agreement would need to include terms for this purpose, including any logistical matters (temporary storage, loading/unloading, chartering or transportation in another manner, e.g., pipeline in the case of gas) and provision to address charges for services rendered.

VI. Interruption or Suspension of Production

13. Notification of interruption or suspension of production

It is conceivable that there might be interruption of production for various reasons including operational decisions (for technical reasons), market conditions (decision taken in response to fluctuating supply, demand and price), bad weather, accidents and possibly *force majeure*. Under what circumstances, if at all, should the ISA be informed by the OCS State of interruptions to production? There is good reason to make such provision, in particular with regard to contributions in kind. The drop in production for the year would result in lower volumes of contributions in kind (and possibly also lower payments depending on market prices). The ISA might have made logistical arrangements that would need to be changed or cancelled.

14. Delay or interruption of payments or contributions in kind

It is conceivable that an OCS State might delay making payments or contributions. Technically, late payments and contributions can constitute breach of Article 82, which may be challenged by other State Parties, because they have to be made on an annual basis. In cases of delay there should be written notice provided to the ISA. A question to consider is whether a coastal State should pay interest on unjustified late payments and contributions, and if so, what procedure to use.

There could be interruption of production for a prolonged period beyond the control of the OCS State. As in the case of the grace period, there is no provision in the Convention to address this situation. In the event of an interruption that lasts several months and possibly a year, the resumed production could be captured by a higher percentage. This could potentially be perceived as an inequitable situation for the OCS State. One way of addressing it is similar to the earlier discussion regarding the grace period, i.e., consider the production year as a 'time account' used for calculation of the applicable rate in a flexible manner. The alternative is to consider suspension of the operation of the Agreement, a situation anticipated by the VCLT 86.[37] In either case, there will need to be provision for notice of delay.[38]

In worst case scenarios, the interruption could be the result of necessity, accident and *force majeure* and it would be unfair to hold the OCS State to the Article 82 obligation without adjustment. It is conceivable that the OCS State is no longer able to perform the obligation, possibly subjecting the agreement to supervening impossibility of performance without the fault of the OCS State, a situation addressed by the VCLT 86.[39] This situation is valid ground not only for suspension but also for premature termination of the Agreement. In all such cases, formal written notice from the OCS State to the ISA should be required as soon as possible.

VII. Monitoring and Confidentiality of Data and Information

---

37   VCLT 86, supra note 11, Art. 57.

38   VCLT 86, ibid., Art. 67.

39   VCLT 86, ibid., Arts. 61-62.

15. Monitoring by the ISA

The provision of data and information by the OCS State to the ISA regarding the basis for the computation of amounts due has already been mentioned. This is in response to a reasonable expectation by the ISA, on behalf of State Parties to the LOS Convention, to ascertain that the amounts received reflect the scale of assessment set out in Article 82(2). There is support in the literature for a provision that would provide the ISA with a monitoring function for this purpose. One author is of the view that the ISA "would need to have a method of verifying production figures submitted to it".[40] The Workshop should consider how such a function might be performed by the ISA or a designate.

16. Confidentiality of data and information

Technical Study No. 4 anticipated that in discharging its responsibilities under Article 82 the OCS State could provide the ISA with confidential or sensitive commercial information. That data could well be subject to ownership rights by operators in the OCS State. The Agreement proposes provisions with regard to explanations for determinations of amounts due by the OCS State and a monitoring function for the ISA. It is reasonable and good practice for the Agreement to include an undertaking on the part of the ISA to maintain confidentiality of information received from the OCS State in discharging its responsibilities.

VIII. Interpretation and Dispute Settlement

17. Good faith

As noted earlier, the duty to perform agreements in good faith is a rule of general international law that is re-stated in the two Vienna Conventions. It is also captured by Article 300 of the LOS Convention and includes an accompanying obligation to exercise rights, jurisdiction and freedoms in a manner that does not constitute an abuse of right. Given the above, is there need for further express provision on good faith in the Model Article 82 Agreement? The argument for inclusion is to establish an express good faith duty for the ISA, which would otherwise be captured only by the VCLT 86 (which is not in force and to which the ISA is not a party) and general international law. The effect would be a more even-handed agreement between the OCS State and the ISA. The choice is between assuming the good faith duty as an implied term and including it as an express term.

18. Interpretation and application consistent with the Convention

A provision in the interpretation clause or later clause will need to situate any interpretative exercise of the Agreement within the framework and object of the LOS Convention. There are useful precedents to consider such as the Straddling Stocks Agreement.[41] The text to include in the Agreement could be to the effect that nothing in the Agreement shall prejudice the rights, jurisdiction and duties of the OCS State and the ISA under the Convention and that the Agreement should be interpreted and applied in the context of and in a manner consistent with the Convention.

19. Applicable law

The Agreement will be governed by the LOS Convention and applicable principles of international law, presumably including principles of equity. The principles of the Vienna Conventions will govern interpretation issues against the backdrop of the LOS Convention.

---

40   George Mingay, "Article 82 of the LOS Convention – Revenue Sharing – The Mining Industry's Perspective," 21 Int. J. of Marine & Coastal L. 335-346 (2006), at 343.

41   Straddling Stocks Agreement, supra note 13, Art. 4.

The parties may need to enter into subsidiary agreements as necessary to achieve the purposes of the Agreement. At least in the case of contributions in kind, there may be need to enter into subsidiary or additional agreements of a commercial nature with the OCS State or designate, such as transportation (chartering and storage) and marketing of the resource in kind. These contractual arrangements will need to have choice of law and forum clauses.

20. Dispute settlement procedures

The discourse regarding the settlement of disputes between States and international organizations is complex.[42] Differences or disputes could arise in the relationship between the OCS State and the ISA. These include differences over the interpretation and application of the Agreement, disagreements regarding the amounts paid against the scale in Article 82(2), unjustified late payments and contributions which entail expense for the ISA, and differences over the extent of the ISA's mandate.

The LOS Convention has made no express provision for the settlement of Article 82 disputes between an OCS State and the ISA. Technical Study No. 4 explained in depth the issues regarding Article 82 dispute settlement.[43] Guidance in dealing with this difficult question in the Model Article 82 Agreement is to be found in part in the VCLT 86 and Annexes, and in a constructive interpretation of particular provisions in the LOS Convention.

First, the Agreement should encourage the parties to resort to an exchange of views and negotiations to resolve differences. In the event of failure to resolve a difference within a specified timeframe, the Agreement could provide for a conciliation procedure between the parties. This procedure is advocated by the VCLT 86 with regard to disputes that do not involve the interpretation of ius cogens.[44]

Second, Article 288 of the LOS Convention anticipates that a court or tribunal shall have jurisdiction over any dispute concerning "the interpretation and application of an international agreement related to the purposes of this Convention, which is submitted to it in accordance with the agreement."[45] A dispute settlement clause in the Agreement would have the effect of a State Party conferring jurisdiction on a court or tribunal. Insofar as the ISA is concerned, the Statute of the International Tribunal for the Law of the Sea (ITLOS) anticipates the possibility that States Parties to the LOS Convention and other entities may confer jurisdiction to it by agreement. It provides that the "Tribunal shall be open to entities other than State Parties ... in any case submitted pursuant to any other agreement conferring jurisdiction on the Tribunal which is accepted by all parties to that case."[46] This is followed by another provision which provides the ITLOS with jurisdiction over "all disputes and all applications submitted to it in accordance with this Convention and all matters specifically provided for in any other agreement which confers jurisdiction on the Tribunal."[47] This is followed further by the following provision:

If all the parties to a treaty or convention already in force and concerning the subject-matter covered by this Convention so agree, any disputes concerning the interpretation or application of such treaty or convention may, in accordance with such agreement, be submitted to the Tribunal.[48]

Technical Study No. 4 interpreted these provisions as enabling an OCS State and the ISA to confer jurisdiction on the ITLOS through a special agreement, or by extension through a provision in the Agreement. Once the ITLOS is seized of the case, the LOS Convention provides for the law to be applied by the Tribunal, namely the LOS Convention and other rules of international law not

---

42   VCLT 86, supra note 11, Art. 66. See Moritaka Hayashi, "The Dispute Settlement Clause of the 1986 Vienna Convention on the Law of Treaties," 19 N.Y.U. J. Int'l L. & Pol. 327 1986-1987.

43   Technical Study No. 4, supra note 2, 64.

44   VCLT 86, supra note 11, Art. 66(4).

45   LOS Convention, supra note 1, Art. 288(2).

46   LOS Convention, ibid., Annex VI, Art. 20(2).

47   LOS Convention, ibid., Annex VI, Art. 21.

48   LOS Convention, ibid., Annex VI, Art. 22.

incompatible with the Convention, and further provides that if the parties so agree, the Tribunal may decide a case *ex aequo et bono*.[49]

In the event that the above provisions cannot be extended to cover an Article 82 dispute, the Assembly and Council of the ISA are empowered to seek an advisory opinion from the Seabed Disputes Chamber of ITLOS "on legal questions arising within the scope of their activities,"[50] which include the ISA's powers with regard to Article 82. The Tribunal's Rules of Procedure provide for advisory opinions referred to it by an international agreement, including a reference by whatever body is authorized by the agreement.[51]

The contractual approach to implementation of Article 82 enables parties to also consider arbitration where conciliation does not resolve differences. It would be useful to consider the model 2010 Arbitration Rules of the United Nations Commission on International Trade Law (UNCITRAL), using the International Bureau of the Permanent Court of Arbitration as forum.[52]

IX. Final Provisions

The provisions in this section are standard clauses in treaties. The Workshop may wish to consider the extent to which, if at all, some of the proposed provisions need to be considered.

21. Duration of agreement

There are two options regarding effective date and duration of the OCS Agreement, both of which track the production life of the deposit, but to different extents.

The first option would see the effective date of the Agreement coinciding with the date of commencement of production in Phase II and would continue until the end of the production life of the resource. This option would include the grace period. A practical consideration for this is that Article 82 technically becomes effective on the date of commencement of commercial production. The computation of the grace period and subsequent scale of payments are based on that date.

The second option would have an effective date coinciding with Phase III, commencing at the start of the sixth year of production and continuing until the end of the production life of the resource. The consideration behind this option is that payments and contributions, which are due on an annual basis, become due only at the end of the sixth year of production, based on production that commences at the start of that year.

There are implications for the rest of the Agreement depending on choice of effective date. With the first option it is conceivable that the first five years of commercial production encounter interruptions which may lead to suspension of production. In that event, it is practical to make provision for possible suspension and eventual resumption of the grace period. The ISA will also need to have a mechanism or process in the Agreement to enable it to monitor the production during the grace period.

22. Amendments

The Agreement should be expected to last as long as commercial production from a site continues. This could be a very long period, perhaps in the order of decades. Unexpected events may arise over the life of the site that might require adjustments to be made to how the relationship between the OCS State and the ISA should be administered. It is advisable to build a capacity to amend the Agreement to address unanticipated matters or simply to ensure that the Agreement remains relevant. Clearly, amendments must continue to be guided by the requirement to ensure consistency with the LOS Convention.

---

49   LOS Convention, ibid., Annex VI, Art. 23 and referentially Art. 293.

50   LOS Convention, ibid., Art 191.

51   International Tribunal for the Law of the Sea, Rules of the Tribunal, Art. 138, online: http://www.itlos.org/fileadmin/itlos/documents/basic_texts/Itlos_8_E_17_03_09.pdf.

52   UNCITRAL, online: http://www.pca-cpa.org/showpage.asp?pag_id=1190.

23. Signature and entry into force

As in other bilateral agreements, the Agreement will have provision for signature and entry into force.

A further consideration is whether the Agreement would benefit from a provision regarding ratification (in the case of the OCS State) where a domestic constitutional requirement so dictates and a consequent act of affirmation (in the case of the ISA). One argument could be that the Agreement does not impose any new international obligations on the OCS State, so that it is effectively a simple executive agreement intended to give effect to an existing conventional obligation. The matter is arguable with regard to the ISA. It may be argued in the latter's regard that as an international organization with full legal personality it is already mandated by its own constitutive instrument to enter into such international agreements and therefore needs no further affirmation. It is also true that the ISA's agreements with contractors with regard to activities in the Area are simply executive agreements that do not require any further act of affirmation. The Agreement could be regarded as another executive agreement. This is a matter for the Workshop to consider.

24. Denunciation

Denunciation is a common term in treaties. It is expressly dealt with in the two Vienna Conventions. It is conceivable that there is no need for such provision in the Agreement as the general international law rules regarding denunciation would apply. However, the Agreement is a somewhat different instrument from other bilateral treaties, in the sense that it does not cover new subject matter and as described earlier, it could be regarded as a form of executive agreement to facilitate the implementation of an existing conventional obligation. Where an OCS State denounces the Agreement, the effect can only be limited to the administrative relationship contemplated in the Agreement to enable implementation of the conventional obligation, but not the conventional obligation itself. For that purpose and greater certainty, it might be useful to include a denunciation clause.[53]

25. Termination

The Model Article 82 Agreement should anticipate how the Agreement may be terminated. A clause on termination should be included.[54] The Agreement could be terminated for several reasons, including: denunciation; end of the production life of a site, either because the resource is depleted or because it is no longer commercially feasible to continue to produce; and prolonged interruption and suspension of production. It is important to anticipate orderly termination of the administrative relationship between the OCS State and the ISA and enable both to complete internal procedures to bring closure. There will need to be notice of termination which should be given at least a year in advance of the effective date of termination (consistent with the duty to make annual payments).

26. Depositary

The designation of depositary is normally important for multilateral instruments rather than for bilateral agreements. However the OCS Agreement is a unique agreement which includes the ISA as a party and acting on behalf of other States Parties to the LOS Convention. The ISA is effectively an ad hoc depositary for such agreements.[55] If the Workshop considers it useful to consider a depositary function for the ISA, the ISA would have a duty to act impartially.[56]

27. Registration and publication

As mentioned earlier, the Agreement is essentially a treaty, albeit between a State and an international organization, and a public document. It should be registered and published with the UN Secretariat.[57]

---

53   VCLT 86, supra note 11, Art. 43.
55   VCLT 86, ibid., Art. 54.
56   VCLT 86, ibid., Art. 77.
56   VCLT 86, ibid., Art. 78.
57   VCLT 86, ibid., Art. 81.

Another reason is that a considerable number of Member States of the United Nations are not parties to the LOS Convention and members of the ISA.

6. CONCLUSION

It is clear that Article 82 of the LOS Convention has textual ambiguities and process gaps that can be expected to constrain implementation. This paper has been prepared to stimulate discussion on how best to address issues. These include the following:

1. This Working Paper distinguishes between issues of interpretation that are essentially administrative and others that may be characterised as substantive in nature.

    a. Are there any substantive issues of interpretation in Article 82 that would require clarification by SPLOS prior to its implementation and if there are, what are they?

    b. If so, in what form (e.g., a resolution of State Parties or more formal agreement)?

2. The Working Paper characterises the relationship between OCS States and the ISA embedded in Article 82 as essentially an administrative one.

    a. Does the Workshop consider the proposed Model Article 82 Agreement to be a useful implementation tool?

    b. What further work does the Workshop recommend be undertaken to further develop the Model Article 82 Agreement?

3. At the Chatham House Workshop participants felt that OCS States should be invited to consider performing their obligation in Article 82 solely through the payment method. The reasons are various: the ISA is not equipped to receive contributions in kind; payments are simpler to administer; implementation/administration costs would be kept to a minimum for both the ISA and OCS State.

    a. Should this idea be pursued further, even though the OCS States have the right to opt for payments or contributions in kind?

    b. If so, should the idea be proposed to SPLOS or simply be discussed with individual OCS States with regard to the content of the Model Article 82 Agreement?

4. In the event that an OCS State opts to make contributions in kind, it is unclear how the obligation is to be discharged and where and how the ISA should be expected to take delivery of the share of the resource contributed.

    a. Is there an expectation that the OCS State will deliver the contribution in kind to a place and time designated by the ISA?

    b. Should the OCS State incur the costs of delivering the contribution or should they be covered in some other manner? If the latter, how?

5. Article 82 does not expressly provide the ISA with an overseeing role as far as the performance of the obligation by the OCS State is concerned. However, it may be implied that the ISA must exercise an administrative monitoring function on behalf of States Parties to enable it to receive payments and contributions in compliance with Article 82(2) and distribute these to other State Parties.

    a. What information should the ISA reasonably expect from OCS States given its responsibilities on behalf of States Parties in Article 82?

    b. What should such a monitoring function be and how far should it go?

    c. How would the ISA perform such a function?

6. The Chatham House Meeting noted that the LOS Convention has not anticipated how disputes regarding the interpretation and application of Article 82 should be resolved. It is conceivable that there could be disputes between States Parties themselves, but these are captured by Article 270 and subsequent provisions. Disputes between an OCS State and the ISA with regard to matters that do not relate to activities in the Area are not expressly captured.

   a. Where an Agreement is entered into and in the event of a dispute between an OCS State and the ISA: in addition to resort to negotiations and possibly conciliation, should there be further resort to advisory opinion (including 'binding advisory opinion') of the ITLOS or other third party settlement such as arbitration? If so, is there preference for a third party resolution mode?

   b. Where there is no Agreement between an OCS State and the ISA: what dispute resolution option(s) applies or should apply? Would advisory jurisdiction by means of an ad hoc agreement between an OCS State and the ISA conferring jurisdiction on ITLOS for this purpose be sufficient? If the OCS State does not express consent, what other procedure could the ISA explore?

As a concluding comment, it can be expected that the ISA will incur expenses in the administration of Article 82. Although this is not an issue for the Model Article 82 Agreement per se, it is an important consideration in how the ISA will discharge its administrative responsibilities in the implementation of this provision. Can the ISA charge its overhead costs to the payments and contributions in kind received from OCS States and before distributing benefits? This is a matter for the Workshop to consider.

REFERENCES

(1)   Primary materials

International instruments

Agreement relating to the Implementation of Part XI of the United Nations Convention on the Law of the Sea of 10 December 1982, New York, 28 July 1994, UN Doc. A/RES/48/263, 17 August 1994, online: http://daccessdds.un.org/doc/UNDOC/GEN/N94/332/98/PDF/N9433298. pdf?OpenElement.

Agreement for the Implementation of the Provisions of the United Nations Convention on the Law of the Sea of 10 December 1982 relating to the Conservation and Management of Straddling Fish Stocks and Highly Migratory Fish Stocks, New York, 4 December 1995, UN Doc. A/CONF.164/37, 8 September 1995, online: http://www.un.org/depts/los/convention_agreements/texts/fish_stocks_ agreement/CONF164_37.htm.

Convention on Limitation of Liability for Maritime Claims, London, 19 November 1976, 1456 U.N.T.S. 221.

Declaration of Principles Governing the Sea-Bed and the Ocean Floor, and the Subsoil thereof, beyond the Limits of National Jurisdiction, UN General Assembly Resolution 2749, (XXV), 17 December 1970, UN Doc. A/RES/25/2749, 12 December 1970, online: http://www.un-documents.net/a25r2749.htm.

International Convention on Civil Liability for Oil Pollution Damage, London, 29 November 1969, 973 U.N.T.S. 3.

International Convention on the Establishment of an International Fund for Compensation for Oil Pollution Damage, 18 December 1971, 1110 U.N.T.S. 57.

International Tribunal for the Law of the Sea, Rules of the Tribunal, online: http://www.itlos.org/ fileadmin/itlos/documents/basic_texts/Itlos_8_E_17_03_09.pdf.

United Nations Convention on the Law of the Sea, Montego Bay, 10 December 1982, UN Doc. A/ CONF.62/122, 7 October 1982, online: http://treaties.un.org/doc/Publication/UNTS/Volume%20 1833/volume-1833-A-31363-English.pdf.

Vienna Convention on the Law of Treaties, Vienna, 23 May 1969, UN Doc. A/Conf.39/27; 1155 U.N.T.S. 331, online: http://untreaty.un.org/ilc/texts/instruments/english/conventions/1_1_1969.pdf.

Vienna Convention on the Law of Treaties between States and International Organizations or between International Organizations, Vienna, 21 March 1986, UN Doc. A/CONF.129/15., March 1986, online: http://untreaty.un.org/ilc/texts/instruments/english/conventions/1_2_1986.pdf.

International decisions

Meeting of States Parties to the United Nations Convention on the Law of the Sea, SPLOS/183, 24 June 2008 SPLOS/183, Decision regarding the workload of the Commission on the Limits of the Continental Shelf (CLCS) and the ability of States, particularly developing States, to fulfil the requirements of Article 4 of Annex II to the Convention, as well as the decision contained in SPLOS/72, paragraph (a), online: http://www.un.org/Depts/los/meeting_states_parties/documents/ splos_183e_advance.pdf.

Meeting of States Parties to the United Nations Convention on the Law of the Sea, SPLOS/72, 29 May 2001, Decision regarding the date of commencement of the ten-year period for making submissions to the CLCS set out in Article 4 of Annex II to the United Nations Convention on the Law of the Sea, online: http://daccess-dds-ny.un.org/doc/UNDOC/GEN/N01/387/64/PDF/N0138764. pdf?OpenElement.

United Nations Secretariat, Assessment of Member States' contributions to the United Nations regular budget for 2012, UN Doc. ST/ADM/SER.B/853, 27 December 2011, online: http://www.un.org/ga/search/view_doc.asp?symbol=ST/ADM/SER.B/853.

International cases

Advisory Opinion Concerning the Interpretation of Peace Treaties with Bulgaria, Hungary and Romania (Second Phase), 18 July 1950, I.C.J. Reports 1950, p. 221, online: http://www.unhcr.org/refworld/docid/4023a1fa2.html.

(2) Secondary materials

Aldo Chircop, 'Operationalizing Article 82 of the United Nations Convention on the Law of the Sea: A New Role for the International Seabed Authority?' 18 Ocean Yb 395-412 (2004).

Tariq Hassan, 'Good Faith in Treaty Interpretation', 21 Va. J. Int'l L. 443-481 (1980-1981).

Giorgio Gaja, 'A 'New' Vienna Convention on Treaties between States and International organizations or between International Organizations: A Critical Commentary', 58 B.Y.I.L. 253-269 (1987).

Richard K. Gardiner, Treaty Interpretation (New York: Oxford University Press, 2008).

Michael W. Lodge, 'The International Seabed Authority and Article 82 of the United Nations Convention on the Law of the Sea', 21(3) Int. J. Mar. & Coast. L. 323-333 (2006).

George Mingay, 'Article 82 of the LOS Convention – Revenue Sharing – The Mining Industry's Perspective', 21 Int. J. of Mar. & Coast. L. 335-346 (2006).

Moritaka Hayashi, 'The Dispute Settlement Clause of the 1986 Vienna Convention on the Law of Treaties', 19 N.Y.U. J. Int'l L. & Pol. 327 (1986-1987).

International Seabed Authority, Issues Associated with the Implementation of Article 82 of the United Nations Convention on the Law of the Sea, Technical Study No. 4 (Kingston: ISA, 2009), online: http://www.isa.org.jm/files/documents/EN/Pubs/Article82.pdf.

International Seabed Authority, Non-Living Resources of the Continental Shelf Beyond 200 Nautical Miles: Speculations on the Implementation of Article 82 of the United Nations Convention on the Law of the Sea, Technical Study No. 5 (Kingston: ISA, 2010), online: http://www.isa.org.jm/files/documents/EN/Pubs/TechStudy5.pdf.

Karl Zemanek, 'The Vienna Convention on Treaties between States and International organizations or between International Organizations', United Nations Audiovisual Library of International Law, 2009, online: http://untreaty.un.org/cod/avl/pdf/ha/vclt/vclt-e.pdf.

(3) Websites

Division for Ocean Affairs and the Law of the Sea, online: http://www.un.org/Depts/los/doalos_activities/about_doalos.htm.

International Law Commission, online: http://www.un.org/law/ilc/.

International Seabed Authority, online: http://www.isa.org.jm/.

International Tribunal for the Law of the Sea, online: http://www.itlos.org/.

Oil & Gas UK, online: http://www.oilandgasuk.co.uk/.

Permanent Court of Arbitration, online: http://www.pca-cpa.org/showpage.asp?pag_id=363.

United Nations Commission on International Trade Law, online: http://www.uncitral.org/.

ANNEX

Framework for an Agreement between an OCS State and the International Seabed Authority on the Implementation of Article 82

Part	Provision	Title	Purpose and possible content
Preamble	Preamble	Preamble	Recalling the context and purpose of the LOS Convention;
			Noting the existence and purpose of Article 82;
			Noting further that the OCS State and the ISA are assigned responsibilities for the purposes of the provision;
			Recognizing that the provision does not set out administrative procedures for the discharge of the responsibilities of the OCS State and the ISA; and
			Being mindful in concluding the Agreement of the need to develop an administrative framework and procedures to facilitate the implementation of Article 82.
			Hereby agree as follows:

Part	Provision	Title	Purpose and possible content
I. Use of terms and scope	1	Interpretation	'the Authority': the International Seabed Authority. 'Contribution in kind': meaning a percentage share of the produced resource in accordance with the scale of assessment in Article 82(2). 'Convention': the United Nations Convention on the Law of the Sea, 1982. 'Outer continental shelf': to refer to the seabed and subsoil of the submarine areas beyond the limits of the EEZ of the OCS State and up to the outer limit of the continental shelf as defined in accordance with Article 76 of the Convention. This definition needs to track the text of Article 76. 'Payments': to refer to monies transferred to the ISA for the purposes of the discharge of the obligation. 'Production': to refer to all production of the resource other than any test production and produced resources used in connection with exploitation. This definition has to take into consideration Article 82(2) which qualifies eligible production so as to focus on commercial production. It takes into consideration that 'test production' is not 'commercial production.' It also takes into consideration that a part of the resource, such as gas, may be re-injected into a well to enhance production. It is conceivable that 'commercial production' might require further definition, possibly with reference to marketability of the produced resource or readiness for processing on a sustained basis. 'Resource(s)': to refer to non-living resource(s) of the outer continental shelf. 'Site': to refer to the geographical location of a resource. The definition should ensure that site means the delineated field of the discovered resource, thereby avoiding an interpretation of site that refers to each individual point of extraction, e.g., per well. 'Value': to refer to the monetary value of the produced resource at the well-head in the case of hydrocarbons and extraction in the case of other non-living resources. The history of negotiations at UNCLOS III suggests that this was the meaning intended for value. 'Volume': to refer to the gross production of the produced resource, but excluding test production and production of resources used in connection with exploitation. This definition would need to be consistent with the Article 82(2) reference to "all production".

Part	Provision	Title	Purpose and possible content
II. Convention Duties	2	Duties of OCS State and the ISA	The OCS State shall make payments or contributions in kind in respect of the production from the exploitation of the non-living resources of the outer continental shelf pursuant to Article 82 of the Convention and in accordance with the procedure set out in this Agreement. The ISA will receive payments and contributions in kind in accordance with this agreement.
	3	Notice to be provided to the ISA regarding choice of payments or contributions in kind	The OCS State shall notify the ISA in writing regarding choice between making payments or contributions. Two alternative approaches: (a) The Agreement could provide notice or contain provision regarding the giving of notice by a specified date; or (b) The Agreement may or may not provide for a change of option after first notice is received by the ISA.
III. Provisions Common to both Payments and Contributions in Kind	4	Grace period	The inclusion of a provision on the grace period depends on date of commencement of the Agreement. The grace period is the first five years of production and is free of payments and contributions. Provision for determination of the grace period, i.e., date of commencement. Possible provision regarding potential suspension of grace period for good cause, to be given as soon as is practicable.
	5	Notice of commencement of production to the ISA	The OCS State shall provide the ISA with written notice of expected commencement of production related to the obligation to make payments or contributions, at least a year before the obligation matures. The notice should contain technical information, such as: identification of the producing site; official date of commencement of commercial production and consequent commencement of the grace period; type of non-living resource; value of production; volume of eligible production.

Part	Provision	Title	Purpose and possible content
	6	Determination of amounts of payments and contributions in kind	Statement of scale set out in Article 82(2) based on years of production: Years 1-5: no payments or contributions Year 6: 1% Year 7: 2% Year 8: 3% Year 9: 4% Year 10: 5% Year 11: 6% Year 12: 7% The OCS State certifies that calculations are in compliance with Article 82, and identifies certifying authority. OCS State provides ISA with information and explanations on how the amounts due are calculated.
	7	Calculation of amounts	The basis for calculating amounts due shall be 'all production'. The portion of the resource used in connection with exploitation shall not be included in the calculation. No local taxes or charges shall be levied against the payments and contributions in kind. Provision regarding costs to cover actual services rendered apart from the obligation to make payments or contributions and with the prior consent of the ISA.
	8	Scheme of Payments and Contributions in Kind	Definition of 'annual' for payment cycle purposes. Provision for potential scheme of periodic payments or contributions in kind over the course of the year. Time is of the essence.
IV. Provisions regarding Payments	9	Making of payments	The OCS State shall designate an authorised institution for the making of payments. The ISA shall designate an authorised office to receive payments. Payments to be made in a designated currency. The ISA shall provide banking instructions to the OCS State. The ISA shall issue receipts for payments received. The ISA shall issue an annual receipt and statement of account.

Part	Provision	Title	Purpose and possible content
V. Provisions regarding Contributions in Kind	10	Making of contributions in kind	The OCS State shall designate an authorised institution for the making of contributions in kind.
			The ISA shall designate an authorised office to receive payments.
			Provision regarding how the OCS State will compute the amount of contribution in kind due as a percentage of the volume of eligible production: basis of production; percentage calculated on volume of eligible production.
			Manner of making of contributions in kind to be set out.
			Possible provision regarding scheme for making of contributions in kind.
			The ISA shall issue receipts for contributions received.
			The ISA shall issue an annual receipt and statement of account.
	11	Delivery of contributions in kind	Provision regarding how the ISA is to take delivery without delay (anticipating arrangements regarding time, location, etc.).
			ISA may instruct delivery to a particular location against costs of delivery. Provision for how costs are to be recovered by the OCS State.
	12	Marketing of contributions in kind	Provision for possible marketing of contributions in kind, including buy-back option for the OCS State.
			Provision regarding logistical arrangements and services for fees provided by the OCS State, including pending marketing.
VI. Interruption or Suspension of Production	13	Notification or interruption or suspension of production	OCS State to provide notice in writing to the ISA in cases of interruption or suspension of production, including reasons, as soon as practicable.
	14	Delay or interruption of payments or contributions in kind	OCS State to provide notice in writing to the ISA in cases of interruption or suspension of payments or contributions in kind, including reasons, as soon as possible.
			OCS and ISA to enter into discussions concerning delay or interruption.
			Effect of unjustified delay in making payments and contributions.
			Justified delay (specify what constitutes justified delay, e.g., force majeure interrupting production) and effect of interruption on the applicable rate of payment or contribution.
			Prolonged delay leading to suspension of agreement (see below).
VII. Monitoring and Confidentiality of Data and Information	15	Monitoring by the ISA	The ISA has a duty to monitor payments and contributions. Need for a provision on the scope of this function and how it should be exercised.
	16	Confidentiality of data and information	The ISA will need to provide an undertaking to maintain confidentiality of data and information received by the OCS State.

Part	Provision	Title	Purpose and possible content
VIII. Interpretation and dispute settlement	17	Good faith	Possible provision on good faith in the interpretation and application of the Agreement.
	18	Interpretation and application consistent with the LOS Convention	Nothing in the Agreement shall prejudice the rights, jurisdiction and duties of the OCS State and the ISA under the Convention, and the OCS Agreement should be interpreted and applied in the context of and in a manner consistent with the Convention.
	19	Applicable law	The Agreement will be governed by the LOS Convention and applicable principles of international law. Parties may enter into subsidiary agreements as necessary to achieve the purposes of the Agreement. Where subsidiary agreements are entered into, they continue to be governed by the main agreement.
	20	Dispute settlement procedures	Possible three-tiered approach: Tier 1: In case of differences, the parties should resort to exchange views and negotiation to resolve the matter within a reasonable timeframe. Tier 2: Failing resolution by negotiation, the parties could resort to conciliation (possibly each appointing a conciliator and a third appointed by the other two). Tier 3: Conferment of full jurisdiction to the ITLOS; or for resort to an advisory opinion of ITLOS; or arbitration using the 2010 UNCITRAL Arbitration Rules with the International Bureau of the Permanent Court of Arbitration as forum.
IX. Final provisions	21	Duration of agreement	Two options: (a) Effective date coinciding with the date of commencement of production in Phase II and until the end of the production life of the resource. (b) Effective date coinciding with Phase III, commencing at the start of the sixth year of production and continuing until the of the production life of the resource. There are implications for the rest of the Agreement depending on choice of effective date.
	22	Amendments	Amendment on the basis of mutual agreement, with a process to commence with provision of notice by either party.
	23	Signature and entry into force	The Agreement will have provision for signature and entry into force.
	24	Denunciation	Either party may denounce the Agreement. Denunciation does not affect either party's rights and responsibilities under the LOS Convention.
	25	Termination	Termination as a result of expiry. Provision of a year's written notice of termination if Agreement is to be terminated for some other reason.
	26	Depositary	ISA to have depositary functions?
	27	Registration and publication	Agreement to be registered with the UN Secretariat?

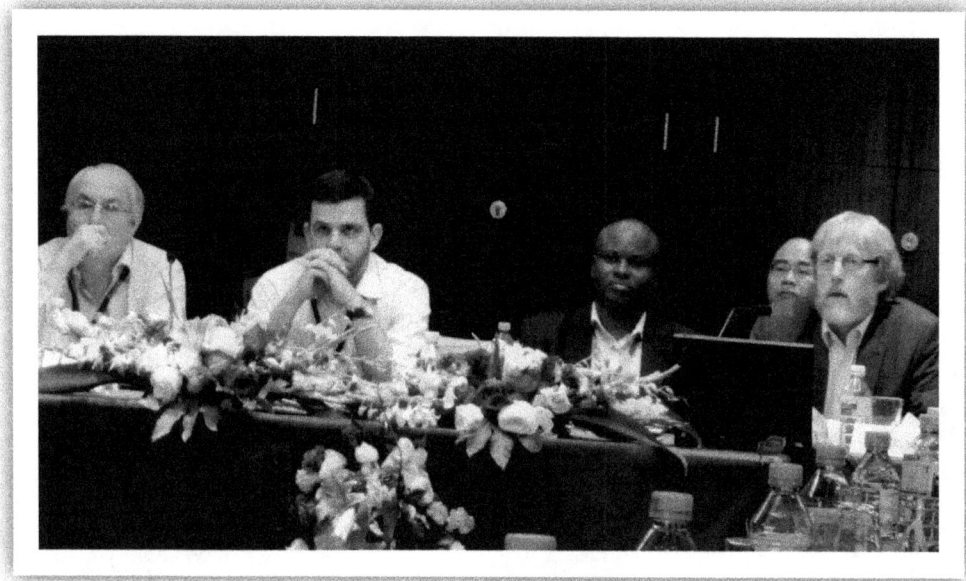

Annex 5:

Working paper on Exploring the Outer Continental Shelf by Professor Clive Schofield, Director of Research, Australian National Centre for Ocean Resources and Security, University of Wollongong, Australia, and Robert van de Poll, International Manager, Law of the Sea, Fugro, N.V., Leidschendam, the Netherlands

EXPLORING THE OUTER CONTINENTAL SHELF

WORKING PAPER

Clive Schofield and Robert van de Poll

Prepared for the International Workshop on Further Consideration of the Implementation of Article 82 of the United Nations Convention on the Law of the Sea, 1982, Beijing, 26-30 November 2012

October 2012

EXPLORING THE OUTER CONTINENTAL SHELF

WORKING PAPER

Clive Schofield[1] and Robert van de Poll[2]

This paper is prepared for the International Workshop on Further Consideration of the Implementation of Article 82 of the United Nations Convention on the Law of the Sea,[3] 26-30 November 2012, Beijing, China.

Abstract

Half of the world's coastal States have moved to secure jurisdictional rights over broad areas of continental shelf seawards of their 200 nautical mile limits. These extensive areas of what are often termed 'outer continental shelf' offer considerable potential resource opportunities, notably with respect to various types of seabed energy resources, seabed minerals and marine genetic resources. This paper provides an overview of progress towards the establishment of outer continental shelf limits, with respect to seabed resource exploration within the Asia-Pacific region in particular. Future challenges concerning the resolution of overlapping claims to areas of outer continental shelf and concerning governing and managing resource-related activities in such areas are also highlighted.

1   Director of Research, Australian National Centre for Ocean Resources and Security, University of Wollongong, Australia. E-mail: clives@uow.edu.au

2   International Manager, Law of the Sea, Fugro N.V., Leidschendam, The Netherlands. E-mail: rvandepoll@fugro.com

3   United Nations Convention on the Law of the Sea, Dec. 10, 1982, 1833 U.N.T.S. 397 (hereinafter LOSC).

1. INTRODUCTION

Recent years have witnessed an enormous expansion in the scope of maritime areas subject to jurisdictional claims on the part of coastal States. In particular this has occurred as coastal States located on broad continental margins have sought to secure their sovereign rights over continental shelf areas located seawards of their 200 nautical mile (nm) exclusive economic zone (EEZ) limits.[4]

These extensive areas of what are often termed the 'outer' or 'extended' continental shelf[5] offer considerable potential resource opportunities. This is particularly the case with respect to seabed energy resources of various types where outer continental shelf areas and the deep and ultra deep water plays that they comprise are set to offer the 'next frontier' for the oil and gas industry over the next 25 years. Seabed resource opportunities relating to minerals (seabed mining) and marine genetic resources are also likely to arise in outer continental shelf areas. These developments are being facilitated by significant advances in drilling and exploration technology allowing for exploration to advance into ever deeper waters and further offshore. Accordingly, it is anticipated that billions of dollars will be devoted to deep sea exploration efforts in the foreseeable future, including of outer continental shelf areas, with trillions of dollars of resources at stake.

This paper provides an overview of current (as of October 2012) progress towards the establishment of outer continental shelf limits on a global basis.[6] Overlaps between submissions are also highlighted. The remainder of the paper narrows the focus to the Asia-Pacific region (broadly conceived). The paper illustrates outer continental shelf submissions and overlaps in the Asia-Pacific and provides a preliminary, indicative assessment of selected outer continental shelf resource exploration opportunities within this region. In this context it is worth noting that coastal States are increasingly offering exploration concessions at or beyond the 200 nm limit. The paper goes on to highlight some of the key future challenges concerning securing outer continental shelf rights and resources, notably in terms of the challenges related to the resolution of overlapping claims to areas of outer continental shelf and concerning governing and managing resource-related activities in such areas.

2. RESEARCH APPROACH

The analysis presented here is fundamentally based on the information provided by coastal States in either their full submissions or submissions of preliminary information to the United Nations Commission on the Limits of the Continental Shelf (CLCS).[7] This information was incorporated into the Fugro Global Law of the Sea (LOS) Database, developed and compiled by the first author of this paper.

This compilation database features: complete global coastlines and borders at 1:75,000 scale, global Landsat TM7 coverage (~2000-2005, 14.25m resolution), Etopo5/Etopo2/Etopo1 bathymetric raster images (2,000m), GEBCO1 bathymetric raster images (2,000m), seismic-derived sediment thickness (fine ~ offshore waters and coarse ~ onshore and offshore) raster images (2,000m), free-air gravity raster images (2,000m) and single-beam (c.24 million nautical miles of data) and multi-beam bathymetry at various resolutions together with the Fugro global cable database. The database also includes territorial sea baselines for all 155 coastal States and agreed maritime boundary

---

4   It is acknowledged that technically the correct abbreviation for a nautical mile is "M" and that "nm" properly refers to nanometres. However, "nm" is widely used by many authorities (for example the UN Office of Ocean Affairs and the Law of the Sea) and appears to cause less confusion than "M", which is often assumed to be an abbreviation for metres.

5   Neither of the terms "outer" or "extended" continental shelf are ideal or have gained universal acceptance. The term "outer continental shelf" suggests that there are distinct parts of the continental shelf when legally this is not the case (see below). For its part the term "extended continental shelf" gives a somewhat misleading impression that coastal States are somehow extending or advancing claims to additional areas of continental shelf. This is not the case as the sovereign rights enjoyed by the coastal State over the continental shelf are inherent. See, LOSC, Article 77(3) and the Judgment of the International Court of Justice in the North Sea Continental Shelf Cases (ICJ Reports, 1969, 3, at para.19). For convenience the "outer continental shelf" will be used in this paper.

6   The paper builds on previous joint work by the authors, notably papers presented at the Advisory Board on the Law of the Sea (ABLOS) conferences in 2010 and 2012. See, for example, Van de Poll, R. and Schofield, C.H. (2010) 'A Seabed Scramble: A Global Overview of Extended Continental Shelf Submissions', Proceedings of the Advisory Board on the Law of the Sea (ABLOS) conference on Contentious Issues in UNCLOS – Surely Not?, International Hydrographic Bureau Monaco, 25-27 October 2010, available at, <http://www.gmat.unsw.edu.au/ablos/ABLOS10Folder/S8P3-P.pdf>.

7   See the CLCS website at, <http://www.un.org/Depts/los/clcs_new/clcs_home.htm>.

delimitation lines, predominantly derived from official sources such as national gazettes. Where the location of territorial sea baselines was absent or otherwise unavailable they were hypothesized and, similarly, theoretical (strict) equidistance lines have been applied for all undelimited maritime boundaries. As indicated above the database also incorporates information included in the submissions made to the CLCS.

Whilst every effort has been made to ensure the accuracy of the figures included in this paper, it should be noted that they are generally not official figures but are instead an independent assessment. It is also worth noting that with respect to many preliminary submissions the precise extent of the areas of outer continental shelf subject to submission is as yet unclear. Whilst the analysis here is based on publically available information most notably that contained in the full submissions and submissions of preliminary information made by the States involved to the CLCS and a rigorous, geodetically robust approach has been applied, the calculations summarised here are necessarily preliminary in nature and are yet to be finalised. It is requested that the figures contained in this paper and accompanying presentation are not quoted without the permission of the authors.

3. GLOBAL OVERVIEW OF OUTER CONTINENTAL SHELF SUBMISSIONS

Of the 193 United Nations member States, 155 are coastal states.[8] Among these coastal States, 78 had, at the time of writing (October 2012), made either full submissions or submissions of preliminary information as a prelude to making full submissions to the CLCS regarding outer continental shelf rights. In total, 100 outer continental shelf submissions had been deposited with the UN, comprising 61 full submissions and 39 preliminary submissions.[9]

These submissions collectively encompass an enormous area, of approximately 29,417,052 km². This figure does not, it is important to note, include outer continental shelf areas for Chile, China, the Comoros and Vanuatu as these States have yet to supply any indication of the extent of their areas of continental shelf located seawards of the 200 nm limit from their baselines.

As coastal States have made their submission it has become clear that numerous overlapping claims to the same areas of outer continental shelf exist. These overlaps encompass approximately 3,227,110 km² of potential outer continental shelf areas.[10] Further, the process is not yet at an end, as a further seven more States are likely to (or may yet decide to) make submissions in due course but have yet to do so because the deadline for their submissions has yet to pass. The States that have yet to make submissions are: Canada, Ecuador, Liberia, Morocco, Peru, USA and Venezuela.[11]

Therefore, as many as 85 coastal States may ultimately be in a position to make submissions for outer continental shelf rights to the CLCS.[12] The overall area of potential outer continental shelf subject to submissions, as well as overlaps between submissions, is therefore likely to increase substantially from the figures provided above as further submissions for outer continental shelf rights are delineated.

---

8   The figure of 155 coastal States includes three States, Azerbaijan, Kazakhstan and Turkmenistan, whose only coastlines are those on the Caspian Sea. Arguably therefore, as the Caspian is not connected to the world ocean save via rivers and canals, this figure could be put at 152 coastal States. For the purposes of this analysis, the more inclusive figure of 155 coastal States is used.

9   Noting that a number of these submissions are joint or partial and these figures are inclusive of multiple partial submissions for different areas by some States. In addition, preliminary submissions are gradually being replaced by full submissions. Thus, while the CLCS lists 45 submissions of preliminary information, only 39 States are involved. See the CLCS website at, <http://www.un.org/Depts/los/clcs_new/clcs_home.htm>.

10   This figure represents an increase as compared with that reported in 2010 of ~2,711,107km² indicating an increase in the number of overlapping submissions deposited with the CLCS.

11   It is worth noting that some of these States are more likely to make submissions than others. For example, Canada's preparations towards formulating a submission are known to be well advanced. Other States that appear to be hemmed in by the maritime entitlements of neighbouring States such as Peru may, nonetheless, opt to make submissions in due course. A submission from the USA presupposes that the USA will eventually become a party to LOSC.

12   This analysis is founded on 2009 Fugro Global LOS Database as compiled by the first author of this paper based on notification and/or analysis.

4. ASIA-PACIFIC SUBMISSIONS

For the purposes of this paper the term 'Asia-Pacific' is taken to mean the broad geographical area bordering the Asian continent fronting onto the Indian Ocean, as well as the western Pacific Ocean including East and Southeast Asia. Some coverage of outer continental shelf issues pertaining to the Pacific Island States and Oceania is also included (see accompanying slides).

Accordingly, there are 51[13] coastal States within the overall Asia-Pacific Regional setting and covered by the present analysis, of which 41 are parties to LOSC.[14] Of 140 potential maritime boundaries in the region 51 have been agreed, leaving 89 (or 63.6 per cent) unresolved or in dispute. This study focuses on 17 coastal States in the Asia-Pacific region, which have collectively made 13 full submissions and four preliminary submissions to the CLCS.

These have been made by: Bangladesh ($\sim$102,069km^2), Brunei ($\sim$ 8,044 km^2 preliminary information $\sim$ no map provided), China (preliminary information $\sim$ no map provided), Federated States of Micronesia ($\sim$211,615km^2 preliminary information), India (two areas $\sim$598,201 km^2), Indonesia (partial, 4,547km^2), Japan (five areas, $\sim$741,572km^2), Malaysia (joint with Vietnam (south), 43,313km^2), Maldives (two areas, $\sim$172,032km^2), Myanmar ($\sim$144,527km^2), Pakistan ($\sim$55,844km^2), Palau (three areas $\sim$258,385km^2), Papua New Guinea (2 areas $\sim$ 202,212 km^2), Philippines (partial, 132,223km^2), Republic of Korea (preliminary information, $\sim$18,636km^2), Sri Lanka ($\sim$1,726,787km^2), Vietnam (North), 12,464km^2).

Collectively these submissions encompass 4,432,471 km^2 of potential outer continental shelf areas.

5. ASIA-PACIFIC OVERLAPS

The above-mentioned submissions include substantial areas of outer continental shelf included in more than one submission. These potential overlaps between submissions are systematically illustrated in the graphics accompanying this paper. They can, however, be summarised as existing between Pakistan and India (19km^2), Maldives and Sri Lanka (9,426 km^2), Sri Lanka and India (345,370 km^2), India and Bangladesh (144,527 km^2), India and Myanmar (121,070 km^2), Bangladesh and Myanmar (100,235 km^2), Brunei and Malaysia and Vietnam (8,044 km^2), Japan and Palau (229,934km^2), Japan and China in the East China Sea,[15] Japan and the Republic of Korea (concerning the southern part of their joint development area in the East China Sea, 18,636km^2), Federated States of Micronesia and Papua New Guinea (193,760 km^2).

In addition, possible future overlapping outer continental shelf issues may arise in the South China Sea if, indeed, any outer continental shelf exists in this area, between Brunei, China, Malaysia, the Philippines and Vietnam.[16] In all, potential overlaps encompass approximately 1,171,021 km^2, equating to 26.4 per cent of outer continental shelf areas submitted involving 16 of the 17 States reporting claimed areas. These significant areas of overlap between submissions are likely to pose coastal States significant challenges with respect to finalizing their outer continental shelf limits, let alone accessing seabed resources within the areas of outer continental shelf concerned (see below).

---

13 This analysis is founded on 2009 Fugro Global LOS Database as compiled by the first author of this paper based on notification and/or analysis based on two of the regional compilations (that is, those for Asian and Oceania) as stored within the Fugro Global LOS database.

14 See United Nations, Status of the United Nations Convention on the Law of the Sea, of the Agreement relating to the implementation of Part XI of the Convention and of the Agreement for the implementation of the Convention relating to the conservation and management of straddling fish stocks and highly migratory fish stocks, New York, updated to 20 September 2011, available at <http://www.un.org/Depts/los/reference_files/status2010.pdf>.

15 This is despite the fact that the East China Sea is less than 400 nautical miles broad and the littoral States claim 200 nautical mile breadth exclusive economic zones. The preliminary submissions of both China and the Republic of Korea therefore relate to areas of continental shelf that are beyond 200 nm from their own baselines but are within 200 nm of Japan's baselines. See, Schofield, C.H. and Townsend-Gault, I. (2010) 'Choppy Waters Ahead in a "sea of peace, cooperation and friendship"?: Slow Progress Towards the Application of Maritime Joint Development to the East China Sea', Marine Policy, doi:10.1016/j.marpol.2010.07.004.

16 Outer continental shelf areas only exist in the South China Sea if the South China Sea disputed islands are considered to be "rocks" within the meaning of Article 121(3) of LOSC, and are thus prohibited from generating continental shelf and exclusive economic zone rights. See, Bateman, S. and Schofield, C.H. (2009), 'Outer Shelf Claims in the South China Sea: New Dimension to Old Disputes', RSIS Commentary (Singapore: S.Rajaratnam School of International Studies (RSIS), 1 July).

6. NEW RESOURCE FRONTIERS

Claims to maritime jurisdiction also often tend to be viewed in resource access terms. Indeed, part of the rationale and justification for the significant expenditure required to formulate outer continental shelf submissions has generally been strongly linked to the potential value of the marine resources contained within these necessarily remote from shore areas of continental shelf. In this context it can be recalled that with regard to the continental shelf, including areas of outer continental shelf, coastal States exercise sovereign rights over these areas "for the purpose of exploring it and exploiting its natural resources".[17]

Of particular interest to many coastal States, especially in the context of rising global energy security concerns, is the possibility that outer continental shelf areas may hold considerable seabed hydrocarbon resources. The deep seabed also has the potential to offer a range of other mineral and biological resources, which are increasingly being exploited, aided by considerable advances in technologies applicable to exploring deep sea areas. The following section highlights some of the potential outer continental shelf resource opportunities with particular reference to oil and gas, gas hydrates and marine genetic resources. This section should be read in conjunction with the accompanying presentation graphic, which serves to illustrate key resource opportunities and developments in this regard.

It has been suggested that the technological developments mentioned above will prompt significant investments, measured in hundreds of billions of dollars, in deepwater exploration to access seabed resources of various types. At stake are seabed resources speculatively estimated in the trillions of dollars. Indeed, in 2000 one study on behalf of the International Seabed Authority (ISA) estimated the potential of eight non-living resources (including oil and gas as well as gas hydrates) within the outer continental shelf worldwide at an astounding US$11,934 trillion.[18] It is worth noting that this figure is at June 2000 commodity prices. Given the general rise in resource commodity prices since that date, it can be plausibly suggested that the equivalent adjusted current figure is considerably higher.

Deep and ultradeep water oil and gas exploration

Offshore areas are an established and increasingly important source of non-living resources such as hydrocarbons, especially in the context of dwindling near and on-shore reserves, growing populations and generally, therefore, resource and energy demands. Indeed, it has been estimated that of the order of one third of global crude oil is located offshore.[19] Increasing reliance on offshore sources of supply is likely to be reinforced in the foreseeable future as oil prices rebound in response to plateauing and declining production (especially but not exclusively from terrestrial oil fields) coupled with increasing demand.

These factors will tend to make the business case for further offshore exploration in deeper, more hostile and challenging waters more persuasive. Given the limited exploration opportunities both onshore and in shallow waters, deep and ultradeep water exploration is also likely to become increasingly important simply in order to offset declining production from existing fields. It is also the case that such areas offer the potential for 'world class', multibillion-barrel discoveries;[20] something that is increasingly unlikely in better prospected on shore and shallow water provinces.[21] Indeed, the already 'spectacular' growth of this sector has been predicted to continue with global capital expenditure on deepwater developments forecast at US$232 billion over the 2012-2016 period – a figure that is 90 per cent more than the amount spent in the preceding five years.[22]

---

17   LOSC Article 77(1).

18   Murton, M.J., Parsons, L.M., Hunter, P. And Miles, P. (2000) "Global Non-Living Resources on the Extended Continental Shelf: Prospects at the Year 2000", ISA Technical Study, No.1, available at, <http://www.isa.org.jm/files/documents/EN/Pubs/TechStudy1.pdf>. See also, Lavoix, H. (2012) "The Deep-Sea Resources Sigils Brief", Red Team Analysis, 1 June 2012, available at, <http://www.redanalysis.org/2012/06/01/the-deep-sea-resources-sigils-brief/>.

19   See, for example, the Rio Ocean Declaration, p.6, available at <http://www.unesco.org/new/fileadmin/MULTIMEDIA/HQ/SC/pdf/pdf_Rio_Ocean_Declaration_2012.pdf>.

20   Such as the 8 billion barrel plus Lula (Tupi) field off Brazil.

21   Harbour J. (2012) 'World Deepwater Market Report 2012-2016', 239.6 (June 2012) Pipeline and Gas Journal 89, 90.

22   Ibid.

Improved technology is increasingly allowing economically viable exploration and exploitation of offshore oil and gas resources in more hostile conditions, including deeper waters (up to and beyond 3,000m depth) further offshore.[23] Dramatic technological advances in the oil and gas industry in recent years, particularly in respect of exploration in deep (that is, water depths in excess of 1,000 feet) and ultradeep (over 5,000 feet) water offshore areas.[24] This has involved the drilling of deeper and deeper wells, for example in the Gulf of Mexico, as well as significant innovations in the design of production platforms and in terms of geophysical exploration technologies, which have significantly enhanced the chances of success in deep seabed exploration and exploitation.[25]

These developments, coupled with high oil prices prior to the onset of the global financial crisis led to substantial growth in deep and ultradeep water drilling so that global deepwater production tripled from approximately 1.5 million barrels per day (b/d) to around 5 million b/d in the period 2000 to 2009. Prior to the Deepwater Horizon disaster in the Gulf of Mexico of 2010, deepwater production was predicted to rise to 10 million b/d by 2015.[26] Indeed, notwithstanding the Deepwater Horizon disaster and its aftermath, deep and ultra deepwater drilling for seabed hydrocarbons are likely to increase significantly in the future, as evidenced by projected capital investment in deep water oil and gas exploration efforts.[27]

The key reason for this is that there is little indication of a sustained move away from global reliance on oil as the primary energy carrier driving the world economy. These mounting energy security concerns are especially pertinent in the Asia-Pacific region where many States are already highly dependent on imported petroleum resources. As oil supplies become increasingly constrained yet demand continues to spiral upwards, there is a high likelihood of increasing oil prices, which in turn will reinforce the case for the exploration for and exploitation of unconventional oil reserves such as deep and ultradeep waters oil reserves.[28]

Although outer continental shelf areas have been generally considered to be of only limited interest to oil companies in the past, there have been indications that such areas may provide seabed oil and gas potential. For example, recent work by Geoscience Australia using advanced aeromagnetic surveys indicates the existence of significant petroleum potential in basins in at least three of Australia's ten areas of outer continental shelf: in the Great Australian Bight to the south, on the Lord Howe Rise to the east and on the Wallaby Plateau off Western Australia.[29]

Of particular note in this context is that presently, at least 13 countries have "issued and/or are offering" offshore oil and gas exploration concession licences beyond their 200nm EEZ limits.[30] These developments may indicate not only a desire by coastal States to 'stake their claims' to outer continental shelf areas but also be symptomatic of a desire by coastal States to yield some return on their investment in terms of going to the expense of formulating submissions on outer continental shelf limits to the CLCS.

---

23   In April 2011 it was reported that the record for the deepest successful drilling had been set at 10,194 feet (3,107m) by ultradeep offshore drillship Dhirubhai Deepwater KG2 off India. See, "Transocean Ltd announces world water depth drilling record in 10,194 feet of water", Transocean New Release, 11 April 2011, available at, <http://phx.corporate-ir.net/phoenix.zhtml?c=113031&p=irol-newsArticle&ID=1549073&highlight=>.

24   The figures of 1,000ft (305m) for deep water and 5,000ft (1,524m) for ultradeep waters are used by the United States government. See, for example, Richard McLaughlin, 'Hydrocarbon Development in the Ultra-Deepwater Boundary Region of the Gulf of Mexico: Time to Reexamine a Comprehensive U.S.-Mexico Cooperation Agreement', 39 Ocean Development and International Law 1-31 (2008), at 1. Other definitions suggest sub-300m water depths as shallow water, 300-1,500m as deep water and 1,500m plus as ultradeep waters.

25   Kelly, P.L. (2004) 'Deepwater Oil Resources: The Expanding Frontier', pp.414-416 in Legal and Scientific Aspects of Continental Shelf Limits, M.H. Nordquist, J.H. More, and T.H. Heidar (eds), (Martinus Nijhoff Publishers): pp.414-416.

26   Owen, N. and Schofield, C.H. (2010) 'Further and Deeper: The Future of Deepwater Drilling in the Aftermath of Deepwater Horizon Disaster', International Zeitschrift, Vol.6, no.3 (December 2010), available at <http://www.zeitschrift.co.uk/>.

27   Harbour, 2012, p.90.

28   Ibid.

29   Cleary, P. (2010) 'Finds fuel deep-sea oil rush', The Australian, 3 April 2010, available at <http://www.theaustralian.com.au/news/nation/finds-fuelbrdeep-seabroil-rush/story-e6frg6nf-1225849081371>.

30   Based on analysis of exploration licenses coupled with 200nm limits.

Gas hydrates are a non-traditional form of seabed hydrocarbons. They comprise ice-like crystalline solids formed from a mixture of water and natural gas, which are stable inside a particular pressure and temperature envelope. It has been conservatively estimated that on a global scale gas hydrates locked in the seabed encompass twice the carbon contained in known coal, oil and natural gas reserves.[31] Accordingly, gas hydrates are the most abundant grade of unconventional natural gas, and are estimated to have a larger resource base than all other grades combined.[32] For example, it has been estimated that Japan alone has gas resources from hydrate deposits in the range of 71-471 trillion cubic feet (tcf) (median estimate of 212 tcf), while the Asia-Pacific as a whole has median estimated gas resources from hydrates of 4,715 tcf of the global estimate of 43,311tcf.[33]

Gas hydrates are particularly attractive as a potential energy resource not only because of their abundance but also because they can deliver substantial energy with more limited release of greenhouse gas emissions compared to 'traditional' energy carriers. For example, methane liberates around 45 per cent more energy when burnt than heavy fuel oil. Further, burning one tonne of heavy oil generates 3.3 tonnes of CO^2 as compared with the 1.24 tonnes of CO^2 generated when one tonne of methane is burnt. Put another way, heavy fuel oil generates 2.66 times more CO^2 as compared to methane. Consequently there are significant potential advantages to substituting gas hydrates for heavy fuel oil. That said, the exploitation of and uncontrolled release of methane from gas hydrate structures (for instance from Arctic regions as a consequence of global warming) poses risks. Land subsidence and landslips on the continental shelf may occur. In addition, it has been suggested that methane is between 10 and 22 times more effective than carbon dioxide in causing climate warming.[34]

It should also be noted that gas hydrates are typically found in two different types of geological setting, that is, either onshore, in and below areas of thick permafrost, or offshore, in the marine sediments of the outer continental margins. The offshore setting where hydrates are liable to occur is directly applicable to outer continental shelf areas, as the gas hydrates are seen to occur in narrow zones, which parallel the sea floor in deeper (500m+) offshore waters.[35]

The commercial production and exploitation of gas hydrates does, however, face significant technical challenges. Consequently, gas hydrates have generally been considered the most difficult and expensive of all unconventional gas resources to recover. This implies that other unconventional gas resources (including tight gas, coal bed methane, and shale gas resources) would be developed in preference to gas hydrates, pushing gas hydrate developments back accordingly.[36]

That said, major oil and gas companies are presently actively engaged in developing solutions to the technical obstacles to the commercial recovery of gas hydrates. Should these efforts prove to be successful, the hydrates located within national jurisdiction, both within and beyond the 200nm limit are likely to be a focus for future exploration efforts. In this context it is worth noting that in May 2012 the completion of a "successful, unprecedented test of technology" resulting in the safe extraction of "a steady flow of natural gas from methane hydrates" was reported.[37] The

---

31 Dillon W. (1992), "Gas (Methane) Hydrates – A New Frontier", U.S. Geological Survey, September 1992, available at, <http://marine.usgs.gov/fact-sheets/gas-hydrates/title.html>.

32 See, Nick A. Owen and Clive H. Schofield, 'Disputed South China Sea hydrocarbons in perspective', Marine Policy, 36 (2012), 809-822, at p.813.

33 Johnson, A.H., (2011), "Global Resource Potential of Gas Hydrate", Hydrate Energy International, 31 August 2011. See also, Research Consortium for Methane Hydrate Resources in Japan (2008) "Japan's Methane Hydrate R&D Program", available at, <http://www.mh21japan.gr.jp/english/wp/wp-content/uploads/ca434ff85adf34a4022f54b2503d86e92.pdf>.

34 Dillon W. (1992), "Gas (Methane) Hydrates – A New Frontier", U.S. Geological Survey, September 1992, available at, <http://marine.usgs.gov/fact-sheets/gas-hydrates/title.html>. See also, Shelander, D., Dai, J., Bunge, G., McConnell, D. and Banik, N. (2010), "Predicting Gas Hydrates Using Prestack Seismic Datain Deepwater Gulf of Mexico", American Association of Petroleum Geologists E-Symposium, 11 February 2010, available at, <http://www.pttc.org/aapg/predictinghydrates.pdf>.

35 While gas hydrates may occur in water depths in excess of 300m, they predominantly occur in the depth range of 500-4,500m.

36 See, Nick A. Owen and Clive H. Schofield, 'Disputed South China Sea hydrocarbons in perspective', Marine Policy, 36 (2012), 809-822, at p.813.

37 United States Department of Energy (2012), "U.S. and Japan Complete Successful Field Trial of Methane Hydrate Production Technologies", 2 May 2012, available at, <http://energy.gov/articles/us-and-japan-complete-successful-field-trial-methane-hydrate-production-technologies>.

project involved collaboration between the US Department of Energy, the Japan Oil, Gas and Metals National Corporation and oil major ConocoPhillips, and involved the injection of a mixture of carbon dioxide and nitrogen into a methane hydrate formation in the North Slope of Alaska, stimulating the production of natural gas.[38] This in situ exchange of CO^2 and nitrogen with methane within a methane hydrate structure offers the potential for carbon sequestration as well as natural gas production.[39] While a small-scale proof of concept experiment, this type of development suggests that the exploitation of hydrate resources, including those located within the outer continental shelf, may not be as far over the horizon as has until recently generally been thought.

Seabed mining

Oil and gas reserves do not constitute the only minerals that can be extracted from the seabed. Indeed, the seafloor has long been the source of valuable resources such as aggregates for building construction and land reclamation, though these have traditionally tended to be accessed from near-shore locations. The scale of extraction can, however, be significant and serve as a source of contention between States.[40] Efforts to exploit other seabed resources such as from placer deposits in marine sediments, including resources such as diamonds and both base metals (such as tin)[41] and precious metals (such as gold and platinum) are also of relatively long-standing. While such efforts have predominantly been undertaken in relatively shallow and thus more readily accessible locations proximate to the coast, and therefore within claimed territorial seas and EEZs, exploration efforts, for example for diamonds, are taking place in progressively deeper waters.[42]

With respect to deep waters (300m and deeper), however, the main seabed mining opportunities generally relate to polymetallic or manganese nodules, ferromanganese nodules and crusts, seafloor massive sulphide (SMS) deposits, cobalt-rich crusts and marine phosphorites. Such deposits also have the potential to contain rare earth elements; something that is likely to enhance their attractiveness as targets for seabed resource development.[43]

While there has been growing interest in deep sea mineral resources such as those that might be derived from manganese and polymetallic nodules in particular since at least the 1960s, especially in the context of the Cold War and elevated concerns over access to so-called 'strategic minerals', the commercial development of such resources has until recently not proved viable. Significant and ongoing advances in deep sea exploration and exploitation technologies, coupled with rising mineral commodity prices, are, however, leading to a reappraisal, and raising the possibility of the viable recovery of a range of resources from the seabed. As a result seabed mining, both within and beyond national jurisdiction, is becoming an increasingly near-at-hand proposition.

Perhaps the most advanced project to date is that related to the exploitation of SMS deposits in the Bismarck Sea off Papua New Guinea. Indeed, Papua New Guinea granted the world's first deep-sea mining lease to Nautilus Minerals Inc. for the development of the Solwara 1 project in January 2011.[44] This project, billed as the world's 'first seafloor gold mine', involves the exploitation of high-grade SMS deposits and hydrothermal sulfide systems in 1,600m of water. Indicated resources for Solwara 1 have been put at 870,000 tonnes of ore containing 6.8 per cent copper and 4.8 grams per tonne of gold, while inferred resources have been put at 1,300,000 tonnes of ore containing 7.5 per cent

---

38   Ibid.

39   Ibid.

40   For example, large-scale extraction of sand from Indonesian islands and waters for export to Singapore for land reclamation purposes led to the imposition of a ban on such exports (from 2007), though the smuggling of illegally mined sand allegedly continued. In particular it was suggested that extensive sand-mining activities, of the order of approximately 300 million cubic meters of sand per annum, had been dredged from the vicinity of one Indonesian island, Pulau Nipa, threatening it with becoming entirely submerged. Reclamation efforts on the part of the Indonesian government subsequently raised and extended the threatened feature. See, Milton, C., "The Sand Smugglers", Foreign Policy, 4 August 2010, available at, <http://www.foreignpolicy.com/articles/2010/08/04/the_sand_smugglers?page=0,1>.

41   Mined offshore Indonesia, Myanmar and Thailand for example.

42   For example diamond mining company De Beers undertakes sea floor mining operations off the Namibian coast in waters of 90-140m depth. See, De Beers, "Marine Mining", available at, <http://www.debeersgroup.com/Operations/Mining/mining-methods/Marine-Mining/>.

43   See, for example, Hein, J. (2012) "Prospects for Rare Earth Elements from Marine Mineral", ISA Briefing Paper, 02/12, May 2012, available at, <http://www.isa.org.jm/files/documents/EN/Pubs/BP2.pdf>.

44   Bashir, M. (2011) 'Deep sea mining lease granted, The Post-Courier, 19 January 2011, available at <http://www.postcourier.com.pg/20110119/news03.htm>. See also the Nautilus Minerals Inc. website available at, <http://www.nautilusminerals.com/s/Home.asp>.

copper and 7.2 grams per tonne of gold together with zinc and silver components.[45] A note of caution is advisable, though, as concerns over environmental impacts coupled with commercial disputes over project funding appear to have led to significant disruption in the progress of the scheme. Nonetheless these developments illustrate the more general potential for such novel developments among the Pacific Island States.[46] Analogous interest in seabed mining, including on areas of outer continental shelf, has been expressed by States such as the Federated States of Micronesia, Japan, Kiribati and Palau (examples provided in accompanying graphics).

Advances in deep-sea resource exploration and exploitation technologies have also given rise to the prospect of accessing seabed resources, not only within areas of outer continental shelf but in deeper waters and areas beyond national jurisdiction. While developments in the Area are proceeding apace, notably in respect of the Clarion-Clipperton Zone in the Equatorial North Pacific Ocean and in the Central Indian Basin of the Indian Ocean,[47] areas of outer continental shelf subject to national jurisdiction are likely to be particularly attractive areas for development from the perspective of the coastal States holding sovereign rights over these areas.

Marine genetic resources from the deep

In addition to mineral and other non-living resources contained in the seabed and subsoil of the outer continental shelf, coastal States also have sovereign rights over "living organisms belonging to sedentary species", defined as "organisms which, at the harvestable stage, either are immobile on or under the seabed or are unable to move except in constant physical contact with the seabed or the subsoil."[48] These sedentary living resources of the outer continental shelf, including marine genetic resources, may also prove to have considerable value.

Marine biota (plants and animals) represent a relatively untapped resource offering developmental potential for a range of valuable applications. Perhaps the best known of these applications are in the medical and pharmaceuticals industries where so called 'wonder drugs' from the sea have been heralded. To date two marine-derived drugs have been approved for use: Prialt®, a painkiller based on cone snail venom peptide omega-conotoxin derived from Conus magnus; and Yondelis®, an anticancer agent derived from sea squirt (trunciate) metabolite ecteinascidilin-743 from Ecteinascidia turbinata.[49] In addition, a host of marine-derived drugs are in development with over 20 candidates undergoing clinical and preclinical trials at the time of writing.[50] Marine-derived products may also have commercial applications in other sectors such as agriculture (providing specialist health foods and dietary supplements as well as agricultural chemicals such as herbicides and pesticides), in the cosmetics industry (for instance the anti-inflammatory properties of the soft coral Pseudopterogorgia elisabethae are used in the Estée Lauder Resilience skin-care range to combat irritation) and in industry, where marine products can provide valuable enzymes and catalysts in industrial processes.[51]

In this context marine species and microorganisms that have evolved to exist in extreme environments (so-called 'extremophiles') are of particular interest. Such environments and habitats include the deep sea, as well as in the vicinity of seamounts, hydrothermal vents and methane seeps. Such features have been discovered on the outer continental shelf. Organisms living here have adapted to survive in the complete absence of light, in conditions of extremely high pressure, in either low or very

---

45   See, Nautilus Cares website at, <http://www.cares.nautilusminerals.com/SubSeaEnvironment.aspx?npath=1,6>.

46   Regarding developments in seafloor polymetallic massive sulphide mining see Herzig, P.M. (2004) 'Seafloor Massive Sulfide Deposits and Hydrothermal Systems', pp.431-456 in Legal and Scientific Aspects of Continental Shelf Limits, M.H. Nordquist, J.H. More, and T.H. Heidar (eds), (Martinus Nijhoff Publishers).

47   For maps detailing areas of exploration as well as information on contractors and reserved areas see the International Seabed Authority (ISA) website at, <http://www.isa.org.jm/en/scientific/exploration>.

48   LOSC, Article 77(4).

49   Skropeta, D. (2011) 'Exploring Marine Resources for New Pharmaceutical Applications', pp.211-224 in Gullett,W., Schofield, C.H. and Vince, J. (eds), Marine Resources Management, (LexisNexis Butterworths, Australia), p.211 and 214-215.

50   Ibid., pp.216-217.

51   Ibid., pp.211 and 217.

high (for example in the vicinity of a hot water vent) temperatures, or in environments characterised by extreme salinity or acidity.

This has led to the emergence of 'bioprospecting' and the deep seabed, including outer continental shelf areas, is likely to be a focus for these activities.[52] This represents a potentially rich resource and opportunity for coastal States. Indeed, marine biotechnology related products were estimated to be worth US$100 billion in the year 2000 alone.[53] The potential for further growth in marine bioprospecting is emphasised by the fact that around 1,000 new marine natural products are reported annually.[54] This points to how biodiversity-rich yet under-explored and thus little known the oceans are. Indeed, it has been suggested that the oceans are 95 per cent unexplored.[55] Moreover, the number of ocean-dwelling species has been estimated at around 10 million – a figure 50 times greater than the number of marine species reported thus far. In this context deep-water areas hold particular promise as they are likely to host unique extremophiles and also because these areas are least explored, notwithstanding the considerable advances in technologies applicable to exploring deep-sea areas made in recent decades.[56] This is illustrated by the fact that of over 30,000 marine natural products reported since the 1960s, less than 2 per cent derive from the deep-sea organisms.[57]

7. FUTURE CHALLENGES

While some progress has been made in the finalisation of outer continental shelf limits in the Asia-Pacific region, it is clear that much remains to be done. Indeed, as noted above, overlapping outer continental shelf claims encompass seabed areas of approximately 3,227,110 square kilometres.

These overlaps give rise to multiple 'new' outer continental shelf boundaries and, it would appear, a proliferation in potential outer continental shelf boundary disputes. The resolution of these disputes and the delimitation of outer continental shelf boundaries remains a key challenge for the coastal States involved as this task is beyond the purview of the CLCS.[58] With respect to realising the marine resource opportunities and benefits potentially arising from rights over areas of outer continental shelf, this is likely to be compromised by overlapping jurisdictional claims. For instance, in the Asia-Pacific region in excess of 26 per cent of the outer continental shelf areas in question are subject to overlapping submissions. This is the case because this scenario deprives commercial entities such as international oil and gas companies of the fiscal and legal certainty that they require in order to invest the billions of dollars necessary to undertake offshore exploration, let alone development, activities in such remote areas that are necessarily far from shore locations.

While practice with respect to the delimitation of outer continental shelf boundaries, and thus the resolution of overlapping claims to outer continental shelf areas, can be regarded as nascent, early indications are that the approach to delimitation within and beyond 200nm limits will be similar. This is supported not only by past State practice but by the International Tribunal on the Law of the Sea (ITLOS) Judgment in the Bay of Bengal Case between Bangladesh and Myanmar.[59] The Bay of

---

52 Bioprospecting has been defined as including "the entire research and development process from sample extraction by publicly funded scientific and academic research institutions, through to full scale commercialization and marketing by commercial interests such as biotechnology companies." See, United Nations, "An Update on Marine Genetic Resources: Scientific Research, Commercial Uses and a Database on Marine Bioprospecting", United Nations Informal Consultative Process on Oceans and the Law of the Sea Eight Meeting, (New York, 25-29 June 2007), p. 7-7. See also, S. Arico and C. Salpin, "Bioprospecting of Genetic Resources in the Deep Seabed: Scientific, Legal and Policy Aspects", UNU-IAS Report, (United Nations University, 2005), pp.25-25, available at <www.ias.unu.edu/binaries2/DeepSeabed. pdf>.

53 Arico and Salpin, "Bioprospecting of Genetic Resources in the Deep Seabed: Scientific, Legal and Policy Aspects": 17, See also, Mossop, J. (2007) 'Protecting Marine Biodiversity on the Continental Shelf beyond 200 Nautical Miles', Ocean Development and International Law 38, pp.283-284, at p.285.

54 Skropeta, 2011: p.217.

55 See, for example, the Rio Ocean Declaration, p.6, available at <http://www.unesco.org/new/fileadmin/MULTIMEDIA/HQ/SC/pdf/pdf_Rio_Ocean_Declaration_2012.pdf>.

56 Ibid., p.221.

57 Ibid.

58 In keeping with LOSC, Article 76(10) the CLCS's recommendations are specifically without prejudice to the delimitation of continental shelf boundaries.

59 Dispute Concerning Delimitation of the Maritime Boundary between Bangladesh and Myanmar in the Bay of Bengal (Bangladesh/ Myanmar), International Tribunal for the Law of the Sea (ITLOS), Case no.16, Judgment, 14 March 2012, available at, <http://www.itlos. org/fileadmin/itlos/documents/cases/case_no_16/1-C16_Judgment_14_02_2012.pdf > [hereinafter Bay of Bengal Case].

Bengal Case provided for the first international judicial delimitation of an outer continental shelf boundary. Although arguments were put forward by Bangladesh in particular on the basis of natural prolongation and geophysical issues, the Tribunal opted to disregard these factors both within and beyond 200nm from the coast. The delimitation line for the EEZ was essentially determined on the basis of the relevant coastal geography.[60] With respect to delimitation of outer continental shelf areas the Tribunal was of the view that, as there is only one continental shelf with no essential difference between those parts of it within and seaward of the 200nm limit, the same delimitation methodology could be applied both within and beyond the 200nm limit. Accordingly, the Tribunal opted to simply continue the delimitation line already delimited for the EEZ beyond the 200nm limit on the same alignment.[61] This suggests that outer continental shelf delimitation will proceed on substantially the same basis as delimitations within the 200nm 'inner' continental shelf/EEZ limit.

Similarly, significant oceans governance challenges arise with respect to outer continental shelf areas, even where no overlapping claims exist. It is worth observing that although much of the debate relating to the outer continental shelf has been concerned with the process by which States can secure their rights over continental shelf areas located seaward of their 200nm limit, this is only the beginning. Once outer continental shelf areas are secured, considerable management and oceans governance responsibilities and challenges in respect of these remote, subsurface seabed areas under national jurisdiction are likely to arise.[62] Coastal States are, however, in a position to draw on the experience of the ISA in the development of its Mining Code for inspiration. Regional approaches may also prove advantageous, as illustrated by the recent drafting of a regional legislative and regulatory framework for deep sea minerals exploration and exploitation for the Pacific African Caribbean Pacific (ACP) States.[63] It is to be hoped that coastal States will apply themselves to addressing these challenges with the same commitment and enthusiasm that they have shown in their efforts to secure outer continental shelf areas.

---

60   Ibid., para. 322.

61   Ibid., para. 449.

62   See, for example, Joanna Mossop, "Protecting Marine Biodiversity on the Continental Shelf beyond 200 Nautical Miles", Ocean Development and International Law 38 (2007).

63   Secretariat of the Pacific Community (2012) Pacific-ACP States Regional Legislative and Regulatory Framework for Deep Sea Minerals Exploration and Exploitation, July 2012.

Author Biographical Notes

Clive Schofield is Professor, Director of Research and ARC Future Fellow at the Australian Centre for Ocean Resource and Security, University of Wollongong, Australia. Prior to this appointment he was Director of Research at the International Boundaries Research Unit, University of Durham, UK. He holds a PhD (Geography) from the University of Durham, UK and an LLM from the University of British Columbia, Canada. He has researched and published primarily on issues related to the delimitation of maritime boundaries, geo-technical issues in the law of the sea, maritime security including maritime piracy and regarding maritime boundary disputes and their resolution. He is co-author (with Professor J.R.V. Prescott) of the book The Maritime Political Boundaries of the World.

Rob van de Poll received his B.Sc. (in Earth Sciences in 1991), and an M.Sc. (Eng) (in Geodesy & Geomatics in 2002). Rob has over 10 years' practical experience working as a field geologist. At CARIS (15 years), he created and developed the CARIS LOTS (Law of the Sea software) for the United Nations. In 2006, Rob joined Fugro Group Worldwide to head up all global operations as International Manager Law of the Sea. Rob developed and manages the Fugro Global Law of the Sea database, used for all Global Law of the Sea projects. It contains ~75 terabytes of public and proprietary digital datasets. To date, Rob has worked on Law of the Sea applications in over 123 of the 155 Coastal States of the World. This involves every aspect of Law of the Sea applications, working with and advising directly to Governments (at Presidential / Prime Ministerial and Ministerial levels), and Industry (Senior Management for Oil & Gas Corporations etc.).

Annex 6:

Working paper on Potential Options on Equitable Distribution of Payments and Contributions by Prof. Frida Armas-Pfirter, Austral University School of Law, Buenos Aires, Argentina

POTENTIAL OPTIONS ON EQUITABLE DISTRIBUTION OF PAYMENTS AND CONTRIBUTIONS

WORKING PAPER

Professor Frida Armas-Pfirter

Prepared for the International Workshop on Further Consideration of the Implementation of Article 82 of the United Nations Convention on the Law of the Sea, 1982, Beijing, 26-30 November 2012

October 2012

I – General Concepts

Article 82 of the United Nations Convention on the Law of the Sea (LOSC, or "the Convention")[1] poses many questions that were dealt with in the Workshop organized by the International Seabed Authority. Throughout my presentation, I only made reference to the potential options for distributing payments or contributions "on the basis of equitable sharing criteria". The purpose of this paper was to serve as a "trigger" for the discussions that were held during the Workshop. For this reason, the main objective was to raise all the questions arising from the application of article 82, paragraph 4, without seeking to solve them, but rather trying to provide useful elements for the discussion, bearing in mind all the factors involved.

Let us begin by quoting the text to be analyzed:

> 82 (4) The payments or contributions shall be made through the Authority, which shall distribute them to States Parties to this Convention, on the basis of equitable sharing criteria, taking into account the interests and needs of developing States, particularly the least developed and the land-locked among them.

Article 82 is clearly one of the results of the negotiations of the Third Conference, as there is no similar provision in the 1958 Geneva Convention on the Continental Shelf.

First, I will refer to the general concepts, which, even though they are not part of paragraph 4 of article 82, are important to an understanding of the spirit of the article.

A) Continental Shelf Concept

The Convention provides a clear definition of what is legally understood by "continental shelf", even when this definition may not be quite accurate from a geological or geophysical point of view.

The continental shelf comprises the seabed and subsoil of the submarine areas that extend beyond the territorial sea of the coastal State throughout the natural prolongation of its land territory to the outer edge of the continental margin, or to a distance of 200 nautical miles (M) from the baselines, where the outer edge of the continental margin does not extend up to that distance.

The elements making up the continental shelf notion are unambiguous:

- The term only refers to the seabed and subsoil of the submarine areas, as the superjacent waters are subject to another legal regime.
- It starts at the outer limit of the territorial sea.
- The typical characteristic of the continental shelf is that it is the "natural prolongation" of the land territory of the coastal State.
- Its natural limit is the outer limit of the continental margin.
- The 200 M limit is supplementary; applying to those cases where the continental margin, due to its geological characteristics, does not extend up to that distance.

The entitlement to the continental shelf is based on the title of the coastal State over the land.[2] The foundation of its rights is mainly "adjacency", as established in the 1958 Geneva Convention on the Continental Shelf.[3]

The International Court of Justice (ICJ), in the 1969 North Sea Continental Shelf Cases, joins the concept of "natural prolongation" to that of "adjacency":

---

[1]   Adopted 10 December 1982, in force 16 November 1994, 833 UNTS 396.

[2]   See. also OUDE ELFERIK, A.G., "The outer limits of the continental shelf beyond 200 nautical miles under the framework of article 76 of the United Nations Convention on the Law of the Sea (LOS)", Presentation in the Seminar on the Establishment of the Outer Limits of the Continental Shelf beyond 200 Nautical Miles under UNCLOS – Its Implications for International Law, Ocean Policy Research Foundation, Tokyo, 2008, pp. 3 and 6.

[3]   Geneva Convention on the Continental Shelf, 1949, Art 1: "the term "continental shelf" is used as referring (a) to the seabed and subsoil of the submarine areas adjacent to the coast but outside the area of the territorial sea, to a depth of 200 metres or, beyond that limit, to where the depth of the superjacent waters admits the exploitation of the natural resources of the said areas; (b) to the seabed and subsoil of similar submarine areas adjacent to the coasts of islands".

> *... that the rights of the coastal State in respect of the area of continental shelf that constitutes a natural prolongation of its land territory into and under the sea exist ipso facto and ab initio, by virtue of its sovereignty over the land, and as an extension of it in an exercise of sovereign rights for the purpose of exploring the seabed and exploiting its natural resources. In short, there is here an inherent right.[4]*

The Court makes it very clear that the coastal State has rights over "the area of continental shelf that constitutes a natural prolongation of its land territory".[5] Of course, the evolution of the legal regime on the continental shelf has always been related to the exploitation of mineral resources, especially hydrocarbons.[6]

This concept of natural prolongation as a basis for the rights over the continental shelf was adopted in article 76 (1) of the Convention.

It is worth noting how the extension of the coastal State's rights over the continental shelf (already been included in the Geneva Convention) were confirmed by the ICJ and definitively established in the Law of the Sea Convention, to become customary law.

The same effectively applies to the definition of the rights of a coastal State over the shelf as exclusive,[7] rather than dependent on occupation or an express proclamation,[8] and inherent. In the Court's words: "the rights of the coastal State in respect of the area of continental shelf . . . exist *ipso facto* and *ab initio*, by virtue of its sovereignty over the land".[9]

Article 77, which reflects the extension of the rights of a coastal State over its continental shelf, is applied to the entire shelf. Even in the case of article 246, when dealing with marine scientific research on the continental shelf, the Convention reiterates that the rights over the continental shelf are the same both inside and outside 200 M. Indeed, even though article 246, paragraph 6 establishes that, beyond 200 M, a coastal State may not withhold consent (except in specifically designed areas), paragraph 7 specifies that this provision is without prejudice to the rights of the coastal State over the continental shelf as established in article 77.[10]

B) "There is in law only a single continental shelf"

These rights, with all their characteristics, apply to the entire continental shelf. In the words of the Arbitral Tribunal between Barbados and the Republic of Trinidad and Tobago: "in any event there is in law only a single 'continental shelf' rather than an inner continental shelf and a separate extended or outer continental shelf"[11]. This statement by the Arbitral Tribunal has been, according to Shabtai Rosenne, "a useful and important clarification".[12] It is worth noting that the Tribunal has stated that

---

4   ICJ, North Sea Continental Shelf Cases (Denmark/Netherlands v. F. R.G.), 1969, paragraph 19, p. 22.

5   Ibid., paragraph 43: "More fundamental than the notion of proximity appears to be the principle ·constantly relied upon by all the Parties · of the natural prolongation or continuation of the land territory or domain, or land sovereignty of the coastal State, into and under the high seas, via the bed of its territorial sea which is under the full sovereignty of that State. There are various ways of formulating this principle, but the underlying idea, namely of an extension of something already possessed, is the same, and it is this idea of extension which is, in the Court's opinion, determinant. Submarine areas do not really appertain to the coastal State because · or not only because · they are near it. They are near it of course; but this would not suffice to confer title, any more than, according to a well-established principle of law recognized by both sides in the present case, mere proximity confers per se title to land territory. What confers the ipso jure title which international law attributes to the coastal State in respect of its continental shelf, is the fact that the submarine areas concerned may be deemed to be actually part of the territory over which the coastal State already has dominion, in the sense that, although covered with water, they are a prolongation or continuation of that territory, an extension of it under the sea. From this it would follow that whenever a given submarine area does not constitute a natural · or the most natural · extension of the land territory of a coastal State, even though that area may be closer to it than it is to the territory of any other State, it cannot be regarded as appertaining to that State; · or at least it cannot be so regarded in the face of a competing claim by a State of whose land territory the submarine area concerned is to be regarded as a natural extension, even if it is less close to it."

6   See Rainer Lagoni, "Oil and Gas Deposits across National Frontiers", The American Journal of International Law, Vol. 73, No. 2 (Apr., 1979), pp. 215-243, and Ted L. McDorman, "The Continental Shelf Beyond 200 Nm: Law and Politics in the Arctic Ocean", in Journal of Transnational Law & Policy, Vol. 18.2, Spring 2009, 155-193.

7   Art. 2 (2) of the Geneva Convention and 77 (2) of LOSC.

8   Art. 2 (3) Geneva Convention and 77 (3) LOSC.

9   ICJ, op. cit, paragraph 19.

10   KIRCHNER, A., "The Outer Continental Shelf: Background and Current Developments", in NDIAYE, T.M., WOLFRUM, R. Law of the Sea, Environmental Law and Settlement of Disputes – Liber Amicorum Judge Thomas A. Mensah, Martinus Nijhoff Publishers, Leyden/Boston, 2007, pp. 602-606.

11   Arbitral tribunal, Barbados v Trinidad Tobago, 2006, paragraph 213 in fine, p. 66.

12   ROSENNE, Shabtai, "Arbitrations under Annex VII of the UNCLOS", in Law of the Sea, Environmental Law, and Settlement of Disputes: Liber Amicorum Judge Thomas A. Mensah, in NDIAYE and Wolfrum (eds), p. 1004.

"although the Parties have used the term 'extended continental shelf', the Tribunal considers that it is more accurate to refer to the 'outer continental shelf', since the continental shelf is not being extended, and will so refer to it in the remainder of this Award".[13]

In turn, the International Tribunal on the Law of the Sea, in the case between Myanmar and Bangladesh, never refers to the "outer" continental shelf. Even though the expression "outer continental shelf" is repeated several times in the award, the Tribunal only uses it when quoting what the parties said.[14]

Instead, the Tribunal took great care in stressing the one and only nature of the continental shelf, both within and beyond the 200 M as a natural prolongation of the coastal State's land territory.

In this spirit, to refer to the part of the continental shelf beyond 200 M as a separate maritime space, with its own entity and its own name ("outer continental shelf") could not be appropriate, even were that name to be used to simplify the identification of such part of the continental shelf.[15] There is an underlying conceptual error in most cases where this term is used. Thus, it would be preferable to avoid the terms "outer continental shelf" or "outer continental States", and simply make reference to the continental shelf beyond 200 M or States whose shelves extend beyond 200 M, as ITLOS does.

Now, if there is a single continental shelf, why are some provisions applied differently based on whether this maritime space is inside or outside 200 M?

These rules need to be understood in the historical context of the negotiations of the Third Conference on the Law of the Sea where a group of States, known as the "broad margin States" or "margineers",[16] acted jointly in matters related to their rights over the continental shelf beyond 200 M.

To this end, it is necessary to first clarify the status of the doctrine and practice regarding the continental shelf when the Conference sessions began in 1973. At that time, the Geneva Convention was in force for more than fifty States and, in addition, many others had effective national legislation acknowledging the Convention's formulae.

Therefore, the exclusive right of a coastal State over the resources of the continental shelf adjacent to its coast, up to 200 meters depth or up to where exploitation was feasible, was widely accepted. This common character had already been acknowledged by the International Court of Justice in the aforementioned judgment.

However, bearing in mind that one of the driving forces of the Conference was the need to consolidate and regulate the deep ocean floor regime as the "common heritage of mankind", it was necessary to clearly establish up to where the coastal States could extend their continental shelves, since where the continental shelf ends, the Area starts, and these two zones have different legal regimes.

The continental shelf is the natural prolongation of the land territory under the sea to the outer edge of the continental margin. Therefore, this maritime space, whether it is inside or outside 200 M, is not part of the Area. In fact, although there is a direct relationship between the extension of the continental shelf and the surface of the Area, there is no "encroachment" on the Area when the limit of the continental shelf is established beyond 200 M. In fact, it is the other way around, as the Area includes the seabed and subsoil beyond the national jurisdiction;[17] therefore, what is considered the natural prolongation of a State's territory cannot be part of the Area.

---

13   Note 4, paragraph 65, p. 14.

14   ITLOS, Case 16 "Dispute concerning Delimitation for the Maritime Boundary between Bangladesh and Myanmar in the Bay of Bengal", Bangladesh/Myanmar, 2012.

15   In the same sense, it would not be appropriate to consider the continental shelf beyond 200 M as a "transitional zone between the areas within the limits of national jurisdiction and the area beyond the limits of national jurisdiction" (Cf. Brown, E.D., The International Law of the Sea, Volume I, Introductory Manual, Dartmouth Publishing Company Limited, Great Britain, 1994, pp. 262-263).

16   Among them: Argentina, Australia, Canada, India, Ireland, New Zealand, Norway, United States, and Uruguay.

17   LOSC Art. 1.1. For the purposes of this Convention: (1) "Area" means the seabed and ocean floor and subsoil thereof, beyond the limits of national jurisdiction.

The outer limit of the continental shelf, as reflected in the Geneva Convention, was indefinite, in the sense that the outer limit could be determined by a fixed distance (at 200 meters depth), but it could also be extended to where the depth of the superjacent waters admitted the exploitation of the natural resources. Consequently, the outer limit could have been determined beyond 200 M. Therefore, even though article 76 specifically defines the possibility to extend the shelf beyond 200 M, it is not clear whether it goes farther than the Geneva Convention's distance.

The fact is that in the negotiations of the Third LOSC Conference, the concept of continental shelf as the natural prolongation of a coastal State's territory was strengthened.

As a result of the negotiations, the States with broad margins were recognized as having a continental shelf up to the outer edge of the continental margin; but the margineers had to make some concessions:

a) The outer limit of the continental shelf had to be determined according to the criteria and restrictions established in article 76, and the scientific information about the outer limit had to be submitted to the Commission on the Limits of the Continental Shelf, which, in turn, had to make recommendations;

b) The revenue from the continental shelf beyond 200 M had to be shared through the ISA, according to article 82.[18]

The scheme of article 82 was a *quid pro quo* in the negotiation package of the continental shelf extension and the alleged "diminution of the resources of the Area", when the different criteria to establish the outer limit were discussed.[19] However, it was always related to the idea of this maritime space as the natural prolongation of a coastal State's territory, and the extent of the rights of a coastal State over its continental shelf beyond 200 M was not being questioned. For example, to be more specific, the Argentine delegation objected the "revenue sharing" concept from the beginning of the negotiations, and withdrew its objections only when it was clearly stated that it was the only way to introduce the Irish formula into the negotiation text.[20]

Consequently, the acceptance of the *quid pro quo* by the margineer States (although it was one of the main concessions they had to make for their proposals to be accepted)[21] did not imply acknowledging that the shelf extending beyond 200 M was part of the Area or that the common heritage of mankind was being reduced.[22] It was always understood that article 82 was not intended

18   See Anderson, D. H.(2009), "The Status Under International Law of the Maritime Areas Around Svalbard", Ocean Development & International Law, 40:373-384; ARMAS-PFIRTER, Frida M. "Submissions on the Outer Limit of the Continental Shelf: Practice to Date and Some Issues of Debate", in VIDAS, Davor (Ed.) Law, Technology and Science for Oceans in Globalisation, Martinus Nijhoff Publishers, Leiden-Boston, 2010, pp. 477-498; TIMO KOIVUROVA "The Actions of the Arctic States Respecting the Continental Shelf: A Reflective Essay", in Ocean Development & International Law, 42:215 and T.L. McDorman, "The Continental Shelf Regime in the Law of the Sea Convention: A Reflection on the First Thirty Years" in The International Journal of Marine and Coastal Law 27 (2012) 743–751.

19   See FLEISCHER, Carl A., "The Continental Shelf beyond 200 Nautical Miles – a Crucial Element in the 'Package Deal': Historic Background and Implications for Today", in VIDAS, Davor (Ed.) Law, Technology and Science for Oceans in Globalisation, Martinus Nijhoff Publishers, Leiden-Boston, 2010, pp. 429-448. See also CHIRCOP, Aldo, "Managing Adjacency: Some Legal Aspects of the Relationship Between the Extended Continental Shelf and the International Seabed Area", in Ocean Development and International Law, 40:4, 2011, pp. 307-316.

20   DAVEREDE, Alberto L. La plataforma continental – Los intereses argentinos en el nuevo derecho del mar, Editorial Universitaria de Buenos Aires, Colección Instituto del Servicio Exterior de la Nación 2, Buenos Aires 1983, p. 89. cfr. pp. 94-95: Of the "margineer" countries, those which most objected to this idea since its beginning were Argentina, Australia and, to a lesser extent, Ireland. (...) The Argentine delegation objected to this concept from the beginning, as mentioned above, not only because of the economic burden imposed on the coastal State, but also because it implies the establishment of a "double regime" for the continental shelf: one up to 200 miles without "revenue sharing", and the other beyond that distance, with "revenue sharing". This threatened the principle of natural prolongation of the land territory, and could have adverse consequences in the early stages of negotiation.

21   The developing States with wide continental shelves tried to be exempted from the payments, but the Conference only agreed to the exception suggested by the Argentine delegation of the countries which imported the mineral in question. Cfr. YTURRIAGA BARBERAN, José Antonio De, Ámbitos de Jurisdicción en la Convención de las Naciones Unidas sobre el Derecho del Mar, Ministerio de Asuntos Exteriores, Madrid, 1996, pp. 280-281, and DAVEREDE, op. cit., pp. 96 and 97: Although Argentina and Australia officially kept their objection to the establishment of the "revenue sharing" system until the last moment, their position was always clearly a minority, and it was weakened from the beginning by the acceptance of the concept by the marginalist States. For this reason, and even without formally accepting the system, the Argentine delegation started (...) working for an exemption in favor of the developing countries which were clear importers of the mineral resources produced in their continental shelves.

22   That is why we do not consider Tonga's reference to Article 82 as 'seem(ing) only to indicate a guilty conscience' to be appropriate, in BROWN, E.D., The International Law of the Sea, Volume I, Introductory Manual, Dartmouth Publishing Company Limited, Great Britain, 1994, p. 146. Quote: UN Press Release SEA/425, 4 March 1981 BROWN, E.D., The International Law of the Sea, Volume I, Introductory Manual, Dartmouth Publishing Company Limited, Great Britain, 1994, pp. 262-263. See CHURCHILL, R.R. & LOWE, A.V., The Law of the Sea, Third Edition, Manchester University Press, Great Britain 1999, pp. 156-157: "The scheme is a kind of quid pro quo for the diminution of the resources of the International Sea Bed Area consequent upon allowing jurisdiction over the shelf beyond the 200-mile limit."

as an application of the "common heritage of mankind" principle, because this principle only applies to Part XI, to the Area and its resources.[23]

The statement of the American report is plain in this sense: "Revenue sharing for exploitation of the continental shelf beyond 200 miles from the coast is part of a package that establishes with clarity and legal certainty the control of coastal States over the full extent of their geological continental margins."[24]

II – Who will distribute the payments and contributions?

When referring to who shall distribute the payments and contributions, paragraph 4 of article 82 is clear: "The payments or contributions shall be made through the Authority".[25]

It is worth noting that this is the only mention to the Authority in the whole article. The preposition is key in this definition: "through the Authority", and not "to the Authority". Actually, the final destination of the payments or contributions is the States Parties and the role of the Authority is only instrumental.[26]

The payments or contributions are resources neither of the Authority nor shared between the coastal State and the ISA or States Parties. This concept is obvious in the United States' commentary to the Convention: "Payments are to be distributed by the Authority to States Parties on the basis of criteria for distribution set out in article 82(4). These funds are distinct from, and should not be confused with, the Authority's revenues from deep mining operations under Part XI. They may not be retained or used for purposes other than distribution under article 82, paragraph 4."[27]

The instrumental role to be fulfilled by the Authority involves the need to analyze the implications of collecting the payments and contributions and then distributing them to States Parties in a timely and efficient manner on its functioning.

This analysis should take into account these possible options:

- The possible additional costs implied by the reception of the payments, especially if they are contributions in kind, and their distribution.
- The origin of the funds used to cover these additional costs: the regular budget of the Authority or a percentage of the amounts collected.

III – Role of the organs of the Authority

The Authority has three main organs: the Assembly, the Council and the Secretariat, and two subsidiary organs: the Legal and Technical Commission and the Finance Committee.[28]

23   International Seabed Authority, Issues Associated with the Implementation of Article 82 of the United Nations Convention on the Law of the Sea, ISA Technical Study No 4, Kingston, Jamaica, pp. 22-24.

24   Roach, J. Ashley and Smith, Robert W., Excessive Maritime Claims, Third Edition, Publications on Ocean Development · Volume 73, Martinus Nijhoff Publishers, Leiden • Boston, 2012, p. 192.

25   During the negotiations there were proposals to designate other UN bodies or regional economic organizations, but in the end the Authority was preferred, as an organization created by the Convention itself.

26   See T.L. McDorman, "The Continental Shelf Regime in the Law of the Sea Convention: A Reflection on the First Thirty Years" in The International Journal of Marine and Coastal Law 27 (2012) 743–751 (751): The ISA, which has a very limited role to play as regards Article 82, being only a recipient of payments or contributions and charged with their distribution to developing States. See also CHIRCOP, Aldo, "Operationalizing Article 82 of the United Nations Convention on the Law of the Sea: a New Role for the International Seabed Authority?", in Ocean Yearbook, Vol. 18, 2004, pp. 395-412.

27   See Roach and Smith, op cit, p. 371: U.S. Commentary, Appendix 8. See Garrett, Hydrocarbons on the Continental Margins: Some of the Issues Addressed in the UNCLOS III Negotiations, in Johnston and Letalik (eds.), The Law of the Sea and Ocean Industry: New Opportunities and Restraints, Proceedings of the Law of the Sea Institute, Sixteenth Annual Conference, June 21–24, 1982, Halifax, Nova Scotia, 420, 422–423, available at http://nsgl.gso.uri.edu/hawau/hawauw82001 /hawauw82001_part13.pdf.

28   The Finance Committee was not established by the LOSC. It was stipulated in the Agreement relating to the Implementation of Part XI of the United Nations Convention on the Law of the Sea of 10 December 1982, adopted 28 July 1994, 33 ILM 1309 (1994 Agreement). It is entrusted with the mission to oversee the financing and financial management of the Authority. The Committee consists of 15 members elected by the Assembly for a period of 5 years taking into account equitable geographical distribution among regional groups and representation of special interests, and has a central role in the administration of the Authority's financial and budgetary arrangements.

The Convention specifically regulates the roles that each main organ has in the distribution of benefits, but, as we will see, this regulation is general in nature, and does not distinguish the origin of those benefits.

First, the Legal and Technical Commission has, in general, powers to make recommendations with regard to the exercise of the Authority's functions upon request of the Council.[29] However, more specifically, as a subsidiary organ of the Council, it is in charge of formulating and submitting to the Council the rules, regulations and procedures related to the distribution of benefits.[30] And once they have been adopted by the main organ, the Legal and Technical Commission has to keep such rules, regulations and procedures under review and recommend to the Council from time to time such amendments thereto as it may deem necessary or desirable.[31]

In turn, the Council's functions include, specifically, recommending to the Assembly rules, regulations and procedures on the equitable sharing of the payments and contributions made by coastal States pursuant to article 82.[32]

Finally, the Assembly has to consider and approve, upon the recommendation of the Council, the rules, regulations and procedures on the equitable sharing of the payments and contributions made pursuant to article 82.[33] It is interesting to note that, if the Assembly does not approve the recommendations of the Council, the Assembly shall return them to the Council for consideration in the light of the views expressed by the Assembly.[34]

The Finance Committee has a role regarding all the activities that could have a financial implication for the Authority. When the 1994 Agreement stipulated its creation, it established that the Assembly and the Council should consider its recommendations regarding, among others, "rules, regulations and procedures on the equitable sharing of financial and other economic benefits derived from activities in the Area and the decisions to be made thereon".[35] Although the payments and contributions in article 82 are not related to the "activities in the Area", a recommendation by the Finance Committee might be useful regarding the criteria for equitable sharing and for setting the reasonable percentage for the Authority to cover the administrative costs related to the reception and distribution of the revenues.

However, for the time being, the rules governing the functioning of the Committee are not related to the content of article 82, as all the funds under its competence are those "of the Authority", or the funds derived from the activities in the Area, which is clearly not the case for those stated in article 82.[36] Any extension of its competences shall expressly be made by the Council.

IV – To whom will the resources be distributed?

Article 82 is unambiguous in establishing that: "(The Authority) shall distribute the payments and contributions to States Parties to this Convention, on the basis (...)".

And article 1 of the Convention specifically defines "States Parties" as "States which have consented to be bound by this Convention and for which this Convention is in force".[37]

---

29   Article 165 (2) (a).

30   Article 165 (2) (f).

31   Article 165 (2) (g).

32   Article 162 (2) (o) (i). These recommendations need to be adopted by consensus, in accordance with Art. 161 (8) (d): "Decisions on questions of substance arising under the following provisions shall be taken by consensus: article 162, paragraph 2(m) and (o)".

33   Article 160 (2) (f) (i). Subparagraph g) also grants the Assembly the power "to decide upon the equitable sharing of financial and other economic benefits derived from activities in the Area", but it must be borne in mind that the funds of Article 82 are not benefits derived from activities in the Area.

34   Article 160 (2) (f) (i) in fine.

35   1994 Agreement, Annex, Section 9 (7). See also Rule 11 (f) of the Rules of Procedure of the Finance Committee.

36   See International Seabed Authority, Technical Study No 4, op. cit, pp. 53-63.

37   LOSC, Art. 1 (2) (1).

Therefore, first it must be considered that all the States Parties – and only they – are the revenue sharing beneficiaries mentioned in article 82. Both requirements – being a State and being a Party – seem logical if related to the origin of article 82 and to the fact that the resources referred to in this article do not come from the common heritage of mankind, but from a negotiation in the framework of a package deal.

On one occasion, it has been implied that, in addition to the States Parties to the Convention, "peoples who have not attained full independence or other self-governing status" should also be considered beneficiaries.[38]

This confusion results from the language used in articles 140, 160 and 162, regarding the functions of the Council and the Assembly. However, a thorough analysis of the context of each rule involved makes it possible to conclude that this is clearly not applied to the distribution of the benefits in article 82.

Indeed, when establishing the Council's functions, article 162 (2) (o) (i) refers, in turn, to any distribution of benefits that the Authority has to make on the basis of "equitable sharing". This subparagraph has two parts: first, it states where those resources to be distributed come from:

a) Financial and other economic benefits derived from activities in the Area.

b) The payments and contributions made pursuant to article 82.

The second part, at the end of the sentence, states the elements to be considered when proceeding to the "equitable sharing": "Taking into particular consideration the interests and needs of the developing States and peoples who have not attained full independence or other self-governing status".[39]

This specification of the beneficiaries is different from the one contained in article 82: "(. . .) taking into account the interests and needs of developing States, particularly the least developed and the land-locked among them".

Effectively, article 162:

a) Does not include a particular consideration of the least developed and land-locked developing States.

b) Mentions peoples who have not attained independence or self-governing status that, of course, are not States Parties as required by article 82. This formulation is almost the same as that of article 140 – the distribution criteria of financial and other economic benefits derived from activities in the Area. This article, while establishing that "The Authority shall provide for the equitable sharing of financial and other economic benefits derived from activities in the Area (…)", specifies that: "Activities in the Area shall (…) be carried out for the benefit of mankind as a whole (…) and taking into particular consideration the interests and needs of developing States and of peoples who have not attained full independence or other self-governing status (…)".

It is important to recall that article 82 is outside Part XI, and it is not related to the whole process of administering the resources that are the common heritage of mankind. The reference to the "peoples" must be considered as being limited to the beneficiaries of the resources of the Area and not increasing the number of beneficiaries of article 82.

The rules involved can be compared for the purposes of clarification:

---

38   See International Seabed Authority, Technical Report No 4, op. cit.

39   As in the case of the Council, in relation with the functions of the Assembly, article 160 deals with the provisions regarding the benefits derived from activities in the Area and the payments and contributions of article 82, so it repeats the general description of beneficiaries, which differs from the one contained in article 82.

Type of resources for which benefit sharing should be determined	Council's role regarding the benefit sharing derived from the resources in both Art. 82 and 140	Assembly's role regarding the benefit sharing derived from the resources in both Art. 82 and 140
LOSC Art. 82: **The payments or contributions** shall be made through the Authority, which shall distribute them to States Parties to this Convention, on the basis of equitable sharing criteria, taking into account **the interests and needs of developing States, particularly the least developed and the land-locked among them.**	LOSC, Art. 162 (o) (i): recommend to the Assembly rules, regulations and procedures on the equitable sharing of financial and other economic benefits derived from *activities in the Area* AND the **payments and contributions made pursuant to article 82**, taking into particular consideration **the interests and needs of the developing States** and *peoples who have not attained full independence or other self-governing status;*	LOSC, Art. 160 (f) (i): to consider and approve, upon the recommendation of the Council, the rules, regulations and procedures on the equitable sharing of financial and other economic benefits derived from *activities in the Area AND* the **payments and contributions made pursuant to article 82**, taking into particular consideration **the interests and needs of developing States** and *peoples who have not attained full independence or other self-governing status.*
LOSC Art. 140: *Activities in the Area* shall (...) be carried out for the benefit of mankind as a whole, irrespective of the geographical location of States, whether coastal or land-locked, and taking into particular consideration *the interests and needs of developing States and of peoples who have not attained full independence or other self-governing status (...)*		

V – Categories of States

We have already seen that the beneficiaries are the States Parties to the Convention. However, the payments or contributions are not going to be distributed evenly. Article 82 establishes that this will be done "on the basis of equitable sharing criteria" and that criterion shall consider:

- The interests and needs of developing States.
- Among those developing States, particularly the least developed and the land-locked.

The category of least developed countries (LDCs) was officially established in 1971 by the UN General Assembly with a view to attracting special international support for the most vulnerable and disadvantaged members of the UN family. They represent the poorest and weakest segment of the international community. They comprise more than 880 million people (about 12 per cent of the world population), but account for less than 2 per cent of world GDP and about 1 per cent of global trade in goods.[40]

The current list of LDCs includes 49 countries (the newest member being South Sudan):[41] 34 in Africa,[42] 14 in Asia and the Pacific and 1 in Latin America. These are: Afghanistan, Angola, Bangladesh, Benin, Bhutan, Burkina Faso, Burundi, Cambodia, the Central African Republic, Chad, the Comoros, the Democratic Republic of the Congo, Djibouti, Equatorial Guinea, Eritrea, Ethiopia, the Gambia, Guinea, Guinea-Bissau, Haiti, Kiribati, the Lao People's Democratic Republic (Lao PDR), Lesotho, Liberia, Madagascar, Malawi, Mali, Mauritania, Mozambique, Myanmar, Nepal, Niger, Rwanda, Samoa, Sao Tome and Principe, Senegal, Sierra Leone, the Solomon Islands, Somalia, Sudan, Timor-Leste, Togo, Tuvalu, Uganda, the United Republic of Tanzania, Vanuatu, Yemen and Zambia.

The list of LDCs is reviewed every three years by the United Nations Economic and Social Council in the light of recommendations by the Committee for Development Policy (CDP). The following three criteria are used by the CDP:

(a) A "low-income" criterion, based on a three-year average estimate of the gross national income per capita.

(b) A "human assets weakness" criterion, involving a composite index (the Human Assets Index) based on indicators of: (i) nutrition (percentage of the population that is undernourished); (ii) health (child mortality rate); (iii) school enrolment (gross secondary school enrolment rate); and (iv) literacy (adult literacy rate).

(c) An "economic vulnerability" criterion, involving a composite index (the Economic Vulnerability Index).[43]

Different thresholds are used in all three criteria to identify cases of addition to and graduation from the list of LDCs. So far, only three countries have graduated from their LDC status: Botswana in December 1994; Cape Verde in December 2007; and the Maldives in January 2011.[44]

In addition to the LDCs, the land-locked States Parties, which were, to a great extent, the driving force behind the adoption of article 82, must be privileged.

---

40   http://www.unohrlls.org/en/ldc/25/

41   http://www.unohrlls.org/en/newsroom/current/?type=2&article_id=230

42   It is expected that African States will particularly benefit in the event of Article 82, because most of the LDCs are from this continent. Cfr. EDWIN EGEDE, "The Outer Limits of the Continental Shelf: African States and the 1982 Law of the Sea Convention", Ocean Development & International Law, 35:157–178, 2004 (158-159).

43   http://www.unohrlls.org/en/ldc/164/

44   Cfr. "The Least Developed Countries United Nations Conference on Trade and Development – Report 2012 (UNCTAD)" at http://unctad.org/en/PublicationsLibrary/ldc2012_en.pdf

Therefore, various situations arise:

1. - Eight States Parties to the Convention can be identified as developing States and, at the same time, least developed and landlocked. These States are:

	State	LDCs	LLS
1	Chad	x	x
2	Lao PDR	x	x
3	Lesotho	x	x
4	Malawi	x	x
5	Mali	x	x
6	Nepal	x	x
7	Uganda	x	x
8	Zambia	x	x

2. - Others, being States Parties and developing States, are either least developed or landlocked:

	STATE	LDCs	LLS
1	Angola	x	
2	Armenia		x
3	Bangladesh	x	
4	Benin	x	
5	Bolivia		x
6	Botswana		x
7	Comoros	x	
8	Democratic Republic of the Congo	x	
9	Djibouti	x	
19	Equatorial Guinea	x	
11	The Gambia	x	
12	Guinea	x	
13	Guinea-Bissau	x	
14	Haiti	x	
15	Kiribati	x	
16	Liberia	x	
17	Macedonia		x
18	Madagascar	x	
19	Mauritania	x	
20	Moldova		x
21	Mongolia		x
22	Mozambique	x	
23	Paraguay		x
24	Samoa	x	
25	São Tomé and Príncipe	x	
26	Senegal	x	
27	Sierra Leone	x	
28	Solomon Islands	x	

	STATE		
29	Somalia	x	
30	Sudan	x	
31	Swaziland		x
32	Tanzania	x	
33	Togo	x	
34	Tuvalu	x	
35	Vanuatu	x	
36	Yemen	x	
37	Zimbabwe		x

Article 82 does not establish any difference between States that have a continental shelf beyond 200 M – and which will consequently contribute to the revenue sharing system – and those that do not.

The table below shows that, among developing or least developed but not landlocked States, some that have made a submission on the outer limit of the continental shelf, so it is possible that they will be obliged to make payments and contributions while at the same time, being beneficiaries of the process.

It is also likely that many coastal States that have made the submission may claim exemption from making payments (article 82, paragraph (3)), as they are net importers of the resources. Should such States benefit *pari passu* with other developing States that do not exploit the continental shelf beyond 200 M? Should the application of an equitable criterion mean that such States are subject to payments at a lower rate? Would be the solution to be adopted be the same if the minerals generating the payments were different from those exported by the State? Finally, should the costs incurred by the coastal State in order to establish the outer limit of its continental shelf beyond 200 M also be taken into account, as this is ultimately what allows it to tap the resources leading to such payments?

The 21 least developed States that have made a submission to the Commission on the Limits of the Continental Shelf (CLCS) are:

	STATE	LDC	Submission
1	Angola	x	x
2	Bangladesh	x	x
3	Benin	x	x
4	Comoros	x	x
5	Democratic Republic of the Congo	x	x
6	Equatorial Guinea	x	x
7	The Gambia	x	x
8	Guinea	x	x
9	Guinea-Bissau	x	x
10	Madagascar	x	x
11	Mauritania	x	x
12	Mozambique	x	x
13	São Tomé and Príncipe	x	x
14	Senegal	x	x
15	Sierra Leone	x	x
16	Solomon Islands	x	x

16	Somalia	x	x
18	Tanzania	x	x
19	Togo	x	x
20	Vanuatu	x	x
21	Yemen	x	x

In summary, we may conclude that:

- Distribution must only be made to States.
- These States must be Parties to the Convention.

When establishing an order of priority or a percentage for distribution, an "equitable sharing criterion" must be used, considering the following:

1. The interests and needs of developing States.

2. ... particularly the least developed and the land-locked. This would pose the following possibilities:

   a) Some States have both characteristics: they are least developed and land-locked; therefore, they would seem to be the first for consideration.

   b) Others have only one of the two characteristics, therefore they could be next, but which of these characteristics would be assigned to one State priority over others?

3. Should the land-locked developed States be privileged over the coastal ones?

Bearing in mind the criteria specified in article 82, the following order of priority might be established when determining the distribution criteria:

1. Developing States that are, at the same time, least developed and land-locked.

2. Developing States that are either least developed or land-locked.

3. Developing States that are not least developed or land-locked.

4. Developed States that are land-locked.

5. Developed States that are not land-locked.

However, it cannot be ignored that there are other elements which are not included in article 82, but which are currently relevant, such as the case of the small island developing States (SIDS), the geographically disadvantaged States, and the newly industrialized States.[45]

Once the priority order by State categories has been solved, other questions will need to be answered, for example: what criterion will be followed to establish a priority? That is, will all of the eight States that are developing, least developed and land-locked be subject to the same percentage, on an equal footing, or should appraisal be included, for example, according to their rank among the least developed States?

In the case of the eight States that are both least developed and landlocked, it is easy to assume that the same proportion may be distributed among all of them. However, the list of developing countries almost reaches one hundred, and among them there are sensible differences to consider. Consequently, it would be suitable to establish some subcategories to facilitate distribution.

Should the distribution criterion involve the calculation of a percentage, in addition to a priority order?

---

45   Some political problems that may arise should also be taken into account, such as in the case of States that have a sovereignty dispute related to the area being exploited, or when there is no recognition of the State or the government.

Will the hierarchy established imply a percentage or an order for distribution?

Should a limit be established to ensure that the amount received by developing States is significant, or should all States be included in the distribution, even when the amounts involved are minimal?

Should a developing State that contributes in the terms of article 82 receive a percentage of its own payment?

A table at the end of this paper details the States meeting the two requirements mentioned in paragraph 4 of article 82, and specifies which have made a submission on the outer limit of the continental shelf.

VI – HOW TO DISTRIBUTE?

The selection of a method of distribution raises many questions.

First, although it is clear that what must be distributed are "the payments and contributions" received by the Authority, should that distribution respect the way in which they have been received? It does not seem practical or reasonable to think that contributions in kind should be distributed as received.[46]

Apart from deciding whether distribution should be made in cash, several other questions are pending regarding, for example, whether distribution will take place annually, and whether a fund is going to be established?

The literal interpretation of article 82, paragraph 4 is that the payments and contributions have to go directly to the States Parties. There is no indication that the funds should be allocated for any particular purpose or to achieve a specific objective.[47] However, does this imply that it could not be done? Is it possible that the reference to "interests and needs" regarding the elements to be taken into account in the distribution may lead to a distribution mode other than the simple transfer of cash? Would it be possible, for example, to create a mechanism that enables the payments and contributions to be used in a way that relates to the objectives, purposes and framework of the Convention? One that, for example, acknowledges the developing States may want to be engaged in the exploitation of the Area, or that establishes programmes or funds to help developing States (especially the least developed and land-locked) to reach the Rio +20 or the Sustainable Development Goals related to oceans? One proposal has been to establish a Common Heritage Fund that could serve as a "holding fund" for the potential distribution of payments and contributions.[48]

VII – CONCLUSIONS

From the above, it is clear that article 82(4) opens up many options for the implementation of payments and contribution, and that the Authority needs to develop and keep updated a set of criteria that may be used to calculate the amounts to be distributed among the States Parties.

The Convention establishes the Council's responsibility to recommend rules, regulations and procedures on the equitable sharing, through the Authority, of the payments and contributions made pursuant to article 82

---

46 The way to handle contributions in kind has been considered in the other papers presented in the Workshop.

47 For example, many States owe several assessed contributions to the Authority. Could a State owe the Authority almost all the assessed contributions and received money from the payments of article 82 without first cancelling the debt?

48 See LODGE, Michael, "The International Seabed Authority and Article 82 of the United Nations Convention on the Law of the Sea", 21 (3) IJMCL, 323-333 (2006). In 1979 the land-locked and geographically disadvantaged States proposed the establishment of a Common Heritage Fund to receive the payments and contributions and then through the Authority for distribution as benefits to developing countries on an equitable basis. See also International Seabed Authority, Technical Report No 4, op.cit., p. 18.

STATE CATEGORIES

	STATE	LEAST DEVELOPED	LANDLOCKED STATE	SUBMISSION TO CLCS
1	Chad	X	X	
2	Lao PDR	X	X	
3	Lesotho	X	X	
4	Malawi	X	X	
5	Mali	X	X	
6	Nepal	X	X	
7	Uganda	X	X	
8	Zambia	X	X	
9	Angola	X		X
10	Armenia		X	
11	Bangladesh	X		X
12	Benin	X		X
13	Bolivia		X	
14	Botswana		X	
15	Comoros	X		X
16	Democratic Rep. of the Congo	X		X
17	Djibouti	X		
18	Equatorial Guinea	X		X
19	The Gambia	X		X
20	Guinea	X		X
21	Guinea-Bissau	X		X
22	Haiti	X		
23	Kiribati	X		
24	Liberia	X		
25	Macedonia		X	
26	Madagascar	X		X
27	Mauritania	X		X
28	Moldova		X	
29	Mongolia		X	
30	Mozambique	X		X
31	Paraguay		X	
32	Samoa	X		
33	São Tomé and Príncipe	X		X
34	Senegal	X		X
35	Sierra Leone	X		X
36	Solomon Islands	X		X
37	Somalia	X		X
38	Sudan	X		
39	Swaziland		X	
40	Tanzania	X		X
41	Togo	X		X
42	Tuvalu	X		
43	Vanuatu	X		X
44	Yemen	X		X
45	Zimbabwe		X	

Appendices

Appendix 1:

International Workshop on Further Consideration of the Implementation of Article 82 of the United Nations Convention on the Law of the Sea

26-30 November 2012
Tangla Hotel, Beijing, China

Programme

Sunday, 25 November 2012

Arrival and Registration at Tangla Hotel, Beijing

Day 1:   Monday, 26 November 2012

8:30-9:00   Registration for participants arriving on 26 November 2012
(Peridot Room, Third Floor, Tangla Hotel)

9:00-9:30   **Opening Session**

Co-Chairs

– *Mr. Michael Lodge, Deputy to the Secretary-General and Legal Counsel, International Seabed Authority (ISA)*

– *Prof. Haiwen Zhang, Deputy Director, China Institute for Marine Affairs (CIMA)*

9:00-9:30   Welcoming Remarks

– *H.E. Mr. Nii A. Odunton, Secretary-General of the ISA;*

– *Mr. Jia Guide, Deputy Director-General, Department of Treaty and Law, Ministry of Foreign Affairs, the People's Republic of China*

– *Prof. Haiwen Zhang, Deputy Director, CIMA*

9:30-10:30   **Session 1: Setting the Scene**

Chair

– *Mr. Michael Lodge, Deputy to the Secretary-General and Legal Counsel, ISA*

9:30-9:50   Introduction of participants

9:50-10:10   Workshop programme and outline, expected results and outcomes

– *Mr. Michael Lodge, Deputy to the Secretary-General and Legal Counsel, ISA*

10:10-10:30   Review of outcomes of 2009 Chatham House seminar

– *Dr. Kening Zhang, Principal Legal Officer, ISA*

10:30-10:35   Group photo

10:35-11:00   Morning tea

11:00-13:00   **Session 2: Status of Resources of the Outer Continental Shelf**

Chair

- *Dr. Kaiser de Souza, Chief, Division of Marine Geology, Geological Survey of Brazil, Ministry of Mines and Energy; Member of the Legal and Technical Commission (LTC), ISA*

11:00-11:30   Status of non-living resources of the OCS

- *Dr. Harald Brekke, Senior Geological and Project Coordinator, Norwegian Petroleum Directorates, Member of the LTC, ISA and former member, Vice-Chairman and Acting Chairman of the Commission on the Limits of the Continental Shelf (CLCS)*

11:30-12:00   Status of submissions to the CLCS and impacts of the submissions on the extent of the Area

- *Dr. Galo Carrera Hurtado, Honorary Consul of Mexico in Nova Scotia and New Brunswick, Canada and Member of the CLCS*

12:00-12:30   Exploring the Outer Continental Shelf

- *Prof. Clive Schofield, Director of Research and ARC Future Fellow, Australian National Centre for Ocean Resources and Security, University of Wollongong, Australia*

13:00-14:00   Lunch

14:00-15:00   **Session 3: Guidelines for the Implementation of Article 82**

Chair

- *Mr. Michael Lodge, Deputy to the Secretary-General and Legal Counsel, ISA*

14:00-14:30   Introduction to working paper on guidelines for the implementation of Article 82 and draft model agreement between ISA and OCS States

- *Prof. Aldo Chircop, Marine and Environmental Law Institute, Schulich School of Law, Dalhousie University, Canada*

14:30-15:00   Canadian experience with regard to royalties from the offshore oil and gas industry

- *Mr. Wylie Spicer, Q.C., Counsel, Norton Rose Canada LLP, Alberta, Canada*

15:30-16:00   Afternoon tea

16:00-17:30   **Session 4: Possible Options for Equitable Distribution of Payments and Contributions and Settlement of Disputes**

Chair

- *H.E. Ambassador Eden Charles, Deputy Permanent Representative of the Republic of Trinidad and Tobago to the United Nations, New York*

16:00-16:30   Presentation on possible options for equitable distribution of payments and contributions

- *Prof. Frida M. Armas-Pfirter, Austral University, Argentina*

16:30-17:00	Settlement of disputes arising from interpretation of the agreement between the ISA and an OCS State

        – *Mr. Aleksander Cicerov, Minister Plenipotentiary, Ministry of Foreign Affairs, Slovenia; Member of the LTC, ISA*

17:00-17:30	General discussion of presentations – 'first reactions'

        Moderator

        – *Mr. Michael Lodge, Deputy to the Secretary-General and Legal Counsel, ISA*

Evening	Welcoming hot-pot dinner by CIMA

Day 2: Tuesday, 27 November 2012

9:00-10:30   Session 5: Case Studies I

        Chair

        – *Mr. Isaac Owusu Oduro, Chief Programme Officer, Programme Planning, Monitoring and Evaluation, Ghana, Accra, Ghana (Member CLCS)*

9:00-9:20	Brazil's practice and experience in its domestic licensing regimes and views on the implementation of Article 82 with regard to its OCS oil and gas activities

        – *Dr. Kaiser de Souza, Chief, Division of Marine Geology, Geological Survey of Brazil, Ministry of Mines and Energy; Member of the LTC, ISA*

        – *Dr. Carlos Alberto Xavier Sanches, Deputy Manager of Government Participation, National Agency of Petroleum, Natural Gas and Biofuels - ANP –Brazil*

9:20-9:40	The Brazilian oil and gas industry royalties

        – *Dr. Carlos Alberto Xavier Sanches, Deputy Manager of Government Participation, National Agency of Petroleum, Natural Gas and Biofuels - ANP –Brazil*

9:40-10:00	United Kingdom's practice and experience in its domestic licensing regimes and views on the implementation of Article 82 with regard to its OCS oil and gas activities

        – *Mr. Christopher Whomersley, Deputy Legal Adviser, Foreign & Commonwealth Office, The United Kingdom*

10:00-10:30	Canada's continental shelf related practices and issues

        – *Prof. Ted McDorman, Legal Bureau, Department of Foreign Affairs and International Trade, Canada / University of Victoria*

10:30-11:00	Morning tea
11:00-13:00	Working Groups

        Working Group A - Implementation guidelines and model Article 82 Agreement

        Facilitator

        – *Prof. Aldo Chircop, Marine and Environmental Law Institute, Schulich School of Law, Dalhousie University, Canada*

Rapporteur

– *Dr. Galo Carrera Hurtado, Honorary Consul of Mexico in Nova Scotia and New Brunswick (Canada), Member of the CLCS*

Working Group B · Recommendations for equitable distribution of payments and contributions

Facilitator

– *H.E. Ambassador Eden Charles, Deputy Permanent Representative, Permanent Mission of the Republic of Trinidad and Tobago to the United Nations, New York*

Rapporteur

– *Mr. Kenneth Wong Counsellor (Commercial) and Trade Commissioner (Education), Embassy of Canada, Beijing, China*

13:00-14:00   Lunch

14:00-15:30   Working Groups (continued)

Working groups A and B

- *Implementation guidelines and model Article 82 Agreement*

- *Recommendations for equitable distribution of payments and contributions*

15:30-16:00   Afternoon tea

16:00-17:30   Session 6: Case Studies II

Chair

– *Mr. Christopher Whomersley, Deputy Legal Adviser, Foreign & Commonwealth Office, The United Kingdom*

16:00-16:30   Norway's practice and experience in its domestic licensing regimes and views on the implementation of Article 82 with regard to its outer continental shelf oil and gas activities.

– *Dr. Harald Brekke, Senior Geological and Project Coordinator, Exploration Department, Norwegian Petroleum Directorates; Member of the LTC, ISA and former member, Vice-Chairman and Acting Chairman of the CLCS*

16:30-17:00   Portugal's practice and experience in its domestic licensing regimes and views on the implementation of Article 82 with regard to its outer continental shelf oil and gas activities.

– *Dr. Pedro Cardoso Madureira, Department of Geosciences, University of Evora, Portugal; Member of the LTC, ISA*

17:00-17:30   Nigeria's practice and experience in its domestic licensing regimes and views on the implementation of Article 82 with regard to its offshore oil and gas activities.

– *Dr. Adesina Thompson Adegbie, Assistant Director, Nigerian Institute for Oceanography and Marine Research, Nigeria; Member of the LTC, ISA*

Evening   Free

Day 3:   Wednesday, 28 November 2012

FIELD TRIP TO TIANJIN CITY

(Information on the trip will be provided to participants upon their arrival in Beijing)

Day 4:   Thursday, 29 November 2012

9:00-10:30   Session 7: Case Studies III

Chair

– *Mr. Satya N. Nandan, Former Secretary-General of the ISA*

9:00-9:30   Japan's practice and experience in its domestic licensing regimes with regard to its CS oil and gas activities and views on implementation of Article 82

– *Mr. Tohru Furugohri, Principle Deputy Director of Ocean Division, International Legal Affairs Bureau, Ministry of Foreign Affairs, Japan*

9:30-10:00   Status of Argentina's submission of OCS claim to the CLCS

– *Prof. Frida Armas-Pfirter, Austral University, Argentina*

10:00-10:30   Ireland's practice and experience in its domestic licensing regimes and views on the implementation of Article 82 with regard to its OCS oil and gas activities

– *Mr. Declan Smyth, Deputy Legal Adviser, Department of Foreign Affairs & Trade, Ireland*

10:30-11:00   Morning tea

11:00-13:00   Working Groups

Working groups A - Implementation guidelines and model Article 82 Agreement

Facilitator

– *Prof. Aldo Chircop, Marine and Environmental Law Institute, Schulich School of Law, Dalhousie University, Canada*

Rapporteur

– *Dr. Galo Carrera Hurtado, Honorary Consul of Mexico in Nova Scotia and New Brunswick (Canada), Member of the CLCS*

Working Group B - Recommendations for equitable distribution of payments and contributions

Facilitator

– *H.E. Ambassador Eden Charles, Deputy Permanent Representative, Permanent Mission of the Republic of Trinidad and Tobago to the United Nations, New York*

Rapporteur

– *Mr. Kenneth Wong Counsellor (Commercial) and Trade Commissioner (Education), Embassy of Canada, Beijing, China*

13:00-14:00   Lunch

14:00-15:30	Working Groups (continued)
	Working groups A, B and C

- *Implementation guidelines and model Article 82 Agreement*
- *Recommendations for equitable distribution of payments and contributions*
- *Procedures for the settlement of disputes*

15:30-16:00	Afternoon tea

16:00-17:30 Session 8: Workshop Outcomes

Chair

- *Mr. Michael Lodge, Deputy to the Secretary-General and Legal Counsel, ISA*

Presentation and consideration of working group outcomes

- *Facilitator/Rapporteur WG A*
- *Facilitator/Rapporteur WG B*

Evening Free

Day 5:   Friday, 30 November 2012

9:00-10:30   Session 8: Workshop Outcomes (continued)

Chair

- *Mr. Michael Lodge, Deputy to the Secretary-General and Legal Counsel, ISA*

9:00 -10:30	Discussion of draft recommendations
10:30-11:00	Morning tea

11:00-13:00   Session 9: Review and Closing

Co-Chairs

- *Mr. Michael Lodge, Deputy to the Secretary-General and Legal Counsel, ISA*
- *Prof. Haiwen Zhang, Deputy Director, China Institute for Marine Affairs (CIMA)*

11:00-12:30	Future work programme, summary and closing
12:30-12:45	Closing remarks by ISA

- *H.E. Mr. Nii A. Odunton, Secretary-General, ISA*

12:45-13:00	Closing remarks by CIMA

- *Prof. Haiwen Zhang, Deputy Director, CIMA*

13:00	Closing lunch hosted by Dr. Huang Huikang, Director General, the Department of Treaty and Law, Ministry of Foreign Affairs, the People's Republic of China, at Tangla Hotel

INTERNATIONAL WORKSHOP ON THE IMPLEMENTATION OF ARTICLE 82 OF THE UNCLOS
《联合国海洋法公约》第82条执行问题国际研讨会
26-30 November 2012   Beijing China
2012年11月26日 30日   中国 北京

Appendix 2:

List of Participants

Dr. Adesina Thompson Adegbie
Assistant Director
Nigerian Institute for Oceanography and Marine Research
P.M.B. 80108
Victoria
Lagos
Nigeria
adeadegbie@yahoo.com; sadegbie@niomr.org

Mr. Neil Adsett
Attorney General
Attorney General's Office
Government of the Kingdom of Tonga
PO Box 85, First Floor, Taumoepeau Building
Corner of Fatafehi and Salote Roads
Nuku'alofa, Kingdom of Tonga
Direct Telephone +(676) 24856
Fax: +(676) 24 005
nadsett@yahoo.com

Mr. Lawrence Apaalse
GNPC, PMB, Tema
Project Coordinator
Ghana National Continental Shelf Delineation Project (GNCSDP)
Tel: +233 22 206020
Cell: +233 243 446338
Apaalse@yahoo.co.uk

Professor Dr. Frida Armas-Pfirter
Austral University School of Law, Buenos Aires, Argentina
Domicilio: Paraguay 1545 - 4° p.
1061 - Ciudad de Buenos Aires
ARGENTINA
Teléfonos: Oficina: 54-11-4819-7611
Celular: 54-911-4972-1567
Frida_Armas@yahoo.com; fza@mrecic.gov.ar

Mr. Harald Brekke
Senior Geological and Project Coordinator
Exploration Department, Norwegian Petroleum Directorates
Technical Advisor to the Norwegian Government on the delineation
of the Norwegian Continental Shelf
Harald.Brekke@npd.no

Mr. Chris G Brown
(Chartered Tax Adviser / Postgraduate LLM in Public Law at University of Cape Town)
Foreign Expert / Teacher
Shandong Jiaotong University
No. 5 Jiaxiao Road
Jinan
Shandong
China 250023
Tel: +86 151 6903 3751 (China)
Tel: +27 (0)83 400 5663 (South Africa)
Tel: +44 (0)1925 261436 (UK)
Email: chrisgbrown@live.co.uk
Skype: chrisgbrown101

Dr. Luis Macias Chapa
Manager of New Business
PEMEX Exploration and Production
Marina Nacional 329, Col. Petróleos Mexicanos,
Miguel Hidalgo, Distrito Federal
Mexico, C.P. 11311
Tel: 19442500 Ext: 32671
Luis.maciasc@pemex.com

Mr. Eden Charles
Deputy Permanent Representative
Permanent Mission of the Republic of Trinidad and Tobago to the United Nations
122 East 42nd Street, 39th Floor
New York N.Y. 10168
U.S.A
trini44@gmail.com

Dr. Aldo Chircop
Professor of Law
Marine and Environmental Law Institute
Schulich School of Law
Dalhousie University
6061 University Avenue
P.O. Box 15000
Halifax, NS, B3H 4R2
Canada
Aldo.Chircop@Dal.Ca

Mr. Aleksander Cicerov
Minister Plenipotentiary
Ministry of Foreign Affairs
Ljubjana
Slovenia
Aleksander.cicerov@gov.si

Miss Fátima de Castro Moreira
University: Portuguese Catholic University - Oporto Law School,
Rua Diogo Botelho 1327 4169-005, Porto, Portugal
Office: Rua do Padrão 198 4150-550 Porto
Home: Rua de Paredes 25 4100-375 Porto, Portugal
fatimacastromoreira@gmail.com

Dr. Kaiser de Souza
Chief
Division of Marine Geology
Geological Survey of Brazil
Ministry of Mines and Energy
Headquarters
SGAN 603
Conj. J, Parte A, 1st floor
70.830-030-Brasflia-DF
Kaisers@df.cprm.gov.br

Dr. Pedro Miguel Ferreira Cardoso Madureira
Department of Geosciences
University of Evora
Largo dos Colegiais 2
7004-516
Evora, PORTUGAL
Pedro@uevora.pt

Mr. Tohru Furuhgori
Principle Deputy Director of Ocean Division
International Legal Affairs Bureau
Ministry of Foreign Affairs, Japan
Bureau tel. +81-3-5501-8333(direct)
Fax:+81-3-5501-8459
tohru.furugohri@mofa.go.jp

Mr. Jia Guide
Deputy Director General
Department of Treaties and Law
Ministry of Foreign Affairs
2 Chaoyangmen Nandajie
Chaoyang District
Beijing 100701
The People's Republic of China
Jia_guide@mfa.gov.cn

Dr. Zhang Haiqi
Director
Department of Geological Investigation
China Geological Survey
45 Fuwai Dajie
Xicheng District
Beijing 100037, The People's Republic of China
Zhanghaiqi@yahoo.cn

Dr. Galo Carrera Hurtado
Honorary Consul of Mexico in Nova Scotia and New Brunswick
130 Lakeshore Park Terrace
Dartmouth, Nova Scotia, Canada
Member
Commission on the Limits of the Continental Shelf
Tel: + (902) 466-3678
Canada B3A 4Z4
gcarrera@ns.sympatico.ca

Mr. Vladimír Jareš
Principal Legal Officer
Administrateur général jurisconsulte
Secretary of the Commission on the Limits of the Continental Shelf
Division for Ocean Affairs and the Law of the Sea
Office of Legal Affairs
United Nations
DC2-0420, New York, NY 10017
phone: (212) 963 3945

fax: (212) 963 5847
jares@un.org; vjares@hotmail.com

Mr. Jiang Jin
Legal Department
China National Offshore Oil Corporation (CNOOC)
P.O.Box 4705
No. Chao Yang Men North Street
Dong Cheng District
Beijing 100010
The People's Republic of China

Mr. Estevao Stefane Mahanjane
Instituto Nacional de Petróleo (INP)
Av. Fernão de Magalhães N° 34, 1°/2°Andar,
P.O. Box 4724
Maputo – Mozambique
Member
Commission on the Limits of the Continental Shelf
Tel. + 258 21 320 935; + 258 82 3081570
+ 258 82 3081870
Fax: + 258 21 320 932
estevao.stefane@inp.gov.mz; stefane7374@gmail.com

Professor Ted McDorman
Legal Bureau
Foreign Affairs and International Trade Canada
Government of Canada
125 Sussex Drive, Ottawa, Ontario, K1A 0G2
Facsimile: (613) 947-7484
Ted.Mcdorman@international.gc.ca
(University of Victoria
Faculty of Law
PO Box 2400 STN CSC
Victoria, British Columbia
Canada, V8W 3H7
tlmcdorm@uvic.ca)

Mr. Satya N. Nandan
Former Secretary-General of the ISA
301 E48th Street #7K
New York, NY 10017
Satya.n.nandan@gmail.com

Mr. Isaac Owusu Oduro
Chief Programme Officer
Programme Planning, Monitoring and Evaluation
Environmental Protection Agency of Ghana
Accra, Ghana
Member
Commission on the Limits of the Continental Shelf
kowusl@yahoo.com

Mr. Marcus Paranaguå
First Secretary
The Sea, Antarctic and Space Division
Ministry of External Relations of Brazil
Marcus.paranagua@itamaraty.gov.br

Dr. Carlos Alberto Xavier Sanches
Deputy Manager of Government Participation
National Agency of Petroleum, Natural Gas and Biofuels · ANP · Brazil
Av. Rio Branco, 65 · 13° andar · Centro
CEP 20090-004 · Rio de Janeiro -RJ
Brazil
csanches@anp.gov.br

Professor Clive Schofield
Director of Research and ARC Future Fellow
Australian National Centre for Ocean Resources and Security
University of Wollongong
Wollongong NSW 2522, AUSTRALIA
ph: +61-2-4221 4446
fax: +61-2-4221 5544
clives@uow.edu.au

Mr. Declan Smyth
Deputy Legal Adviser
Department of Foreign Affairs & Trade
Dublin 2
Tel: 00 353 1 408 2323
Fax: 00 353 1 478 5950
declan.smyth@dfa.ie

Mr. Wylie Spicer, QC
Counsel
Norton Rose Canada LLP
Suite 3700, 400 3rd Avenue SW
Calgary
Alberta
T2P 4H2
CANADA
wylie.spicer@nortonrose.com

Dr. Lu Wenzheng
Second Institute of Oceanography
36 Baochubei Road
Hangzhou 310012
The People's Republic of China
Member
Commission on the Limits of the Continental Shelf
Lu_wenzheng@163.com

Mr. Christopher Whomersley
Deputy Legal Adviser
Foreign & Commonwealth Office
The United Kingdom
Tel: +44 (0)207 008 3284
Fax: +44 (0)207 008 2280
chris.whomersley@fco.gov.uk

Mr. Kenneth Wong
Counsellor (Commercial) and Trade Commissioner (Education)
Embassy of Canada
19 Dongzhimenwai Dajie
Chaoyang District
Beijing, The People's Republic of China 100600
Kenneth.Wong@international.gc.ca

Ms. Yang Xiaoning
Department of Treaties and Law
Ministry of Foreign Affairs
2 Chaoyangmen Nandajie; Chaoyang District
Beijing 100701, The People's Republic of China
Yang_xiaoning@mfa.gov.cn

Mr. Liu Yang
Deputy Director
Department of Treaties and Law
Ministry of Foreign Affairs
2 Chaoyangmen Nandajie; Chaoyang District
Beijing 100701, The People's Republic of China
Liu_yang6@mfa.gov.cn

Dr. Snjezana Zaric
International Cooperation
Programme 'Implementing the UN Convention on the Law of the Sea'
Federal Institute for Geosciences and Natural Resources (BGR)
GEOZENTRUM HANNOVER
Stilleweg 2
30655 Hannover
Germany
Phone: +49 (0)511 643 2991
Fax: +49 (0)511 643 532991
Snjezana.Zaric@bgr.de
www.bgr.bund.de/unclos

ISA Secretariat

Mr. Nii A. Odunton
Secretary-General
International Seabed Authority
14-20 Port Royal Street
Kingston, Jamaica
nodunton@isa.org.jm

Mr. Michael Lodge
Deputy to the Secretary-General and Legal Counsel
International Seabed Authority
14-20 Port Royal Street
Kingston, Jamaica
mlodge@isa.org.jm

Mr. Kening Zhang
Principal Legal Officer
International Seabed Authority
14-20 Port Royal Street
Kingston, Jamaica
kzhang@isa.org.jm

CIMA

Dr. Zhang Haiwen
Deputy Director General
China Institute for Marine Affairs
State Oceanic Administration
1 Fuxingmenwai Avenue
Beijing 100860
The People's Republic of China
haiwen@cima.gov.cn

Ms. Jia Yu
Deputy Director General
China Institute for Marine Affairs
State Oceanic Administration
1 Fuxingmenwai Avenue
Beijing 100860
The People's Republic of China
Jia_yu@cima.gov.cn

Mr. Wu Jilu
Associate Research Fellow
Acting Director
Division for the Law of the Sea
China Institute for Marine Affairs
State Oceanic Administration
1 Fuxingmenwai Avenue
Beijing 100860
The People's Republic of China
jiluwu@cima.gov.cn

ISA TECHNICAL STUDY SERIES

Technical Study No. 1   Global Non-Living Resources on the Extended Continental Shelf: Prospects at the year 2000

Technical Study No. 2   Polymetallic Massive Sulphides and Cobalt-Rich Ferromanganese Crusts: Status and Prospects

Technical Study No. 3   Biodiversity, Species Ranges and Gene Flow in the Abyssal Pacific Nodule Province: Predicting and Managing the Impacts of Deep Seabed Mining

Technical Study No. 4   Issues associated with the Implementation of Article 82 of the United Nations Convention on the Law of the Sea

Technical Study No. 5   Non-Living Resources of the Continental Shelf Beyond 200 Nautical Miles: Speculations on the Implementation of Article 82 of the United Nations Convention on the Law of the Sea

Technical Study No. 6   A Geological Model of Polymetallic Nodule Deposits in the Clarion-Clipperton Fracture Zone

Technical Study No. 7   Marine Benthic Nematode Molecular Protocol Handbook (Nematode Barcoding)

Technical Study No. 8   Fauna of Cobalt-Rich Ferromanganese Crust Seamounts

Technical Study No. 9   Environmental Management of Deep-Sea Chemosynthetic Ecosystems: Justification of and Considerations for a Spatially-Based Approach

Technical Study No. 10   Environmental Management Needs for Exploration and Exploitation of Deep Sea Minerals

Technical Study No. 11   Towards the Development of a Regulatory Framework for Polymetallic Nodule Exploitation in the Area.

ISBN-13: 978-976-8241-17-7

9 789768 241177

www.ingramcontent.com/pod-product-compliance
Lightning Source LLC
Chambersburg PA
CBHW051414200326
41520CB00023B/7231